Past Masters
General Editor Keith Th[...]

Schiller

T. J. Reed is Taylor Professor of the German Language
and Literature at the University of Oxford, and a Fellow
of The Queen's College. He is the author of the Past
Masters volume on *Goethe* (OUP, 1984).

1759 — 1805

Past Masters

T. J. Reed

Schiller

Oxford   New York

OXFORD UNIVERSITY PRESS

1991

Oxford University Press, Walton Street, Oxford OX2 6DP

Oxford New York Toronto
Delhi Bombay Calcutta Madras Karachi
Petaling Jaya Singapore Hong Kong Tokyo
Nairobi Dar es Salaam Cape Town
Melbourne Auckland

and associated companies in
Berlin Ibadan

Oxford is a trade mark of Oxford University Press

First published 1991 as an Oxford University Press paperback

British Library Cataloguing in Publication Data

Reed, T. J. (Terence James) 1937–
Schiller. —(Past masters).
1. Drama in German. Schiller, Fredrich, 1759–1805
I. Title II. Series
823.6
ISBN 0-19-287670-8

Library of Congress Cataloging in Publication Data
Reed, T. J. (Terence James), 1937
Schiller / T. J. Reed.
p.   cm. — (Past masters)
Includes bibliographical references and index.
1. Schiller, Friedrich, 1759–1805.   2. Authors, Germans—18th
century— Biography.   I. Title.   II. Series.
831'.6—dc20   PT2482.R44   1991   [B]   90-7833
ISBN 0-19-287670-8

Typeset by Colset Private Ltd.
Printed in Great Britain by
The Guernsey Press Co. Ltd.
Guernsey, Channel Islands

For Malcolm Pasley

Contents

Note on references

H   refers to the Hanser Verlag edition of Schiller's works in five volumes, edited by Gerhard Fricke and Herbert G. Göpfert, Munich 1958–9. Quotations are by volume (small Roman) and page (Arabic), e.g. iv. 63.

P and D   in the discussion of *Wallenstein*, refer respectively to the second and third parts of the trilogy, *The Piccolomini* and *Wallenstein's Death*.

All Schiller's verse-plays are quoted by line-numbers. Letters are quoted by date and sender and/or recipient. All translations are my own.

Introduction

In a letter of 27 August 1794 confirming their new-found friendship and looking forward to an alliance which would transform
the German literary world, Goethe wrote to Schiller: 'I have
always had a high regard for the rare integrity and seriousness
that are plain in everything you have written and done.' The
simple testimony is easily overlooked amid the wealth of literary insights and projects that crowd the early pages of their
correspondence. Yet Goethe's words go to the core of the man.
High seriousness is the stamp of everything Schiller undertook
and achieved. No writer was ever more committed to the civiliz-
ing purposes of literature, its vital place in the public forum,
its capacity to change human beings and their society. Few can
have argued that case to a greater philosophical depth or with
more passionate eloquence. Perhaps no critic has placed literature in such a grand and coherent framework of historical development and intrinsic values, while at the same time making so
many concise individual judgements that are intuitively persuasive. Certainly no literary legislator ever made greater
demands on poetry and poets—on himself most of all: he
wore out his health meeting them, and died at the age of
forty-six.

The dominant image of Schiller is accordingly that of a tireless crusader, a moral authority, a lofty idealist of whose commitment to truth, goodness and beauty Goethe could later write
in a commemorative poem that it left 'behind him, as a sham
without a substance, The mean banality that tames us all'.
Many of the dramatic characters Schiller created seem to reflect
this. In grim situations they assert elevated values and win
moral victories of a kind at odds with modern pessimistic
assumptions. They make the moral issues explicit and mark the
moment of victory in memorable formulas, which were duly
memorized and much quoted by cultivated people in the nineteenth century and have lived on as increasingly worn common-
places to irritate later, more sceptical generations. Nowhere in

Schiller's work is there successful comedy, and he made few and strictly localized attempts at it.

All this may suggest that Schiller not only led a strenuous intellectual and moral life himself, but will also prove to be a bit of a strain for the reader—that the moral authority will turn out to be a moralizer, the crusader a humourless prig, the idealist short of the necessary realism to make his vision convincing. The answer is that Schiller, though a moralist, is not a moralizer. He can be and has been made to appear one only when the aphorisms that come at climactic points in his dramas are taken, against all the rules of good reading, in isolation from the struggles that give the dramas their substance. There is rarely priggishness because his characters and their situations are realized in accessible and moving terms. The men and women who achieve victories over their circumstances and themselves are shown with none of their human weaknesses hidden, they are not beings of a different world from ours. For them, and for Schiller himself in his poems and essays, ideals by their very nature are enough to keep those who try to achieve them realistic, humble, human. The odds against fulfilling a high aim, and the length of the task that stretches ahead once we are committed to it, are part of his theme. The tone is consequently more often wistful and elegiac than hortatory.

Given all this, it would be premature to rule Schiller's literary idealism out of court. High aspirations do not automatically demand to be ironized, however unfashionable they may have become. Irony is an often necessary salt, but there are some great dishes it must not be allowed to spoil. What is more, Schiller's vision is generous and inclusive. He knows what we need to make us whole, even when—or rather, especially when—it is something that his character or circumstances denied to him personally. Thus he devoted most of his working life to the creation of tragedy, yet in his overall conception of literature he gives the higher place to comedy; for only in the harmonious conclusions that comedy characteristically achieves do we rise above the harshness of mere heroic struggle and taste something of the serenity of the gods (v. 1018). In the same spirit, though his plays and his theoretical essays on drama both focus on the processes of rational reflection and anguished decision, he believes that ethical perfection would—and in rare fortunate individuals does—consist in a spontaneous natural grace of action. Similarly, although by the necessity of cultural history as he saw it he himself was a highly reflective modern writer, he located supreme poetic achievement in distant ages of naïve unselfconsciousness—or, once again, in the rare individuals who had somehow managed to retain or restore in themselves that enviable primal state. More fundamentally still, the essence of all aesthetic experience lay for this earnest mind in the activity of *play* (*Spiel*). That made art the highest and richest of mankind's activities, because human beings only play when they are in the fullest sense human, and they are only fully human when they play (v. 618).

Finally—and most famously, because Beethoven took the young Schiller's words and built them into the climactic choral movement of his last symphony—what may lie beyond all human earnestness and effort is the condition of joy. Not, it is true, a self-indulgent emotion, nor the kind of sublime but still individual sentiment that Wordsworth felt in nature's lonely places, but a generous elation which grows out of the forms of happiness people experience in their separate lives and carries them beyond individuality and social convention into loving community. When he wrote his ode 'To Joy' in 1785, Schiller had been lifted out of despair by the enthusiastic appreciation of a group of young people in Leipzig whom he had never met. It was a moment, rare in his life, when reality seemed briefly less resistant to his efforts, and human warmth and solidarity seemed the norm.

Johann Christoph Schiller was born in 1759 on 10 November (Luther's birthday) in the small town of Marbach in Württemberg, and spent his childhood years in that neighbourhood. His father was a man of humble origins who had begun to learn the surgeon's trade, but then been tempted to 'go for a soldier'. He had seen action as a mercenary (on both sides, by the chance of capture) in the War of the Austrian Succession. He was now a recruiting officer in the service of the Duke of Württemberg and not in easy circumstances, in part because he was sometimes left unpaid. Later, in 1775, he became overseer of the gardens at one of the Duke's new castles, Schloss Solitude. He had an eye for practicalities and an urge to communicate: he wrote books, on agriculture in Württemberg (1769) and on tree-cultivation in general (1795). Both of these works edged beyond the merely practical into the social. The Württemberg economy, half ruined by a succession of spendthrift dukes, could well do with the improved farming practices Johann Kaspar Schiller had observed in the course of his campaigns; and his passion for trees inspired him to address the mighty of his day in forthright terms: 'Your fine houses and gardens are closed to the country people. Recompense them with the sight and enjoyment of a thousand avenues of trees, and their descendants will bless you for it.' By 1789, Johann Kaspar was claiming to have planted some thirty thousand trees and shrubs himself. It is all a gentle portent: the concern for society's welfare, the address to the powerful, and that massed natural growth springing up from within the artificiality of one of the petty courts by which eighteenth-century Germany was divided-and-ruled, together make an apt prelude to the young Schiller's work, which links social rebellion with natural growth and impulse.

These too were being cultivated, though not by design, at Castle Solitude where Schiller was undergoing an education he had not wanted. His reaction to it was eventually to cast him out, with only his genius to support him, on a society neither welcoming to genius nor designed to accommodate it. The 1770s in Germany had seen a revolt by a group of slightly self-conscious literary 'geniuses', the so-called 'Storm and Stress' (*Sturm und Drang*) writers, against literary rules and more substantive social restrictions. But this brief 'genius period', though it beneficially loosened up literature, gained no substantive freedoms. For Schiller, coming a little later, his chosen freedom meant struggling to survive in a harsh environment where literary patronage was hard to come by and where the literary market had not yet developed even the simple institutions like copyright which can make it feasible to live by the pen. And freedom in his case also meant exile from his native duchy and separation from his family and friends, a dismal rootlessness which was hardly relieved by the opportunity it gave him to claim that he was now an Enlightenment cosmopolitan

(v. 855). True, it was exile from a limiting provincialism, a move to a cultural centre that looked more promising and where he had achieved a sensational first success in the theatre. But the promise stayed unfulfilled, the prospects dissolved, the 'centre' finally rejected him There *was* no true literary centre to this fragmented Germany, which was still as far from cultural as from political nationhood. An adequate base from which to create what Schiller had it in him to create was something which itself still had to be created. Helping Goethe to do that was to be one of Schiller's achievements.

Meantime, body and soul had to be kept together by literary makeshifts that stole time from more ambitious projects, hampered the growth of a poet's mind, and used up energies that were not boundlessly renewable. So that by the time Schiller did have a settled centre for his work and was truly free to follow his chosen course, he had just one decade left. It became a decade of intense creative work, matched and stimulated by Goethe's equally intense activity, and given a sense of coherent purpose by their partnership. Schiller wrote his dramatic masterpiece the trilogy *Wallenstein*, four more major plays, numerous adaptations and translations (of Euripides, Shakespeare, Racine), an impressive body of poetry, two great essays in aesthetics and literary criticism, and a correspondence (especially with Goethe and with Wilhelm von Humboldt) which is a mine of insights. All this by stubborn persistence against the ill health that was the legacy of his early struggles. It issued a clear warning as early as 1791, when he suffered months of severe illness.

Highpoint, maturity, and decline thus virtually coincide—or rather, there is no decline, no mellow descent into age after the high plateau of maturity, no late wisdom, no final statement with rich autumnal colouring. Only an abrupt cessation. Like Keats, who wondered whether his pen would ever fully 'glean his teeming brain' and bring the 'full ripened grain' safely in, Schiller consciously worked against time. His image is as striking as the one Keats used, and has an even more urgent note of danger: 'I will do what I can,' he wrote to Goethe on 31 August 1794, 'and when the building collapses I will perhaps have rescued what is worth preserving from the fire.' He died on 9 May 1805. A new historical drama lay partly worked out on his desk.

1 Absolutism and revolt

An education

Schiller was both victim and beneficiary of eighteenth-century absolutism. In 1773, already at the age of fourteen resolved to study theology and train for the Church—the classic start in life of middle-class Swabian intellectuals—he was torn from family, school, and chosen career and placed in the Duke of Württemberg's Academy, the 'Hohe Karlsschule' or 'Karl's High School'. It was the Duke's own doing: Karl Eugen kept an eye open for signs of ability in reports from schools and in chance encounters with his subjects. His offer to educate your son was then a virtual command; a father who declined it risked disfavour and the ruin of his own career. Schiller's father did decline at first, on the ground that the Academy could not offer the theological training his son wanted. It was not in an easy position to do so, as the foundation of a Catholic Duke in a jealously Protestant state, which already had a time-honoured faculty and famous seminary at Tübingen. But the subject's personal preference counted for little. At the third time of asking, already dangerously late, Schiller's father yielded. In return the Duke promised that the boy would be better provided for than any preacher. Schiller was put down to be a lawyer; later he switched to medicine when the new faculty was added, perhaps because of his father's old interest.

Founding his Academy was the most striking act of Karl Eugen's later reign. Being pressed into it was the dominant experience of Schiller's early life. Two forces normally opposed to each other in eighteenth-century society here meet in a paradoxical mixture: on the one hand education, through which Enlightenment thinkers hoped to bring about social change and human fulfilment, and on the other hand arbitrary power, which limited that fulfilment drastically and cried out for change most urgently. Here for once was power promoting education. Which element in the mixture dominated? Was it a truly enlightened absolutism, or was it despotism thinly disguised? The answer matters, not just for our judgement of a not very significant eighteenth-century ruler, but for our judgement of Schiller's in every sense dramatic beginnings and of their place and value in his life's work.

Karl Eugen came to the throne of Württemberg in 1744, aged sixteen and prematurely declared to be of age for the purpose. Over the next twenty-five years he was virtually a caricature of unenlightened absolutism. He strained the resources of his small state so as to emulate the glories of a greater—he had stayed briefly at Louis XV's court in 1748. He spent freely on ballet, opera, festivities, and an army. He built on a grand scale, castles and palaces (seven in one decade) lodges, gardens, and one of the largest opera-houses in Europe. He engaged the best Italian and French dancers, artists, and craftsmen. The Württemberg Estates at first met his demands without demur, which is surprising, since he was continuing a long dynastic tradition of excess. But their resistance grew with his demands and the peremptoriness of his tone (he upbraided them for opposing 'the just commandments and desires of a most gracious father of his people'). Withholding money was the only power the Estates had, not enough to make Württemberg the 'only other constitutional monarchy in Europe', as Charles James Fox called it, but enough to ensure a constant battle between court extravagance and bourgeois obstinacy. Karl Eugen's attempts to bypass the Estates and finance himself from other sources were unsavoury. Treaties at different times with France and Prussia brought him in 'subsidies' in return for an undertaking to provide troops should they ever need them. In effect, he was selling his subjects. The practice was admittedly common enough in eighteenth-century Germany. So was the perception of a fundamental opposition underlying the financial conflict, namely that between pious bourgeois rectitude and cynical court immorality. The Duke filled the conventional role exactly: his female artistes often did double duty; contemporaries numbered his mistresses in treble figures, colour-coded shoes for the current favourite helped keep track of a fast-changing situation. More seriously, justice was flouted and corrupted. People were imprisoned for being personally or politically inconvenient: a singer who revealed an early *affaire* of the Duke's to his wife was held for ten years; a rival of the Duke's Minister Count Montmartin for four years, on the evidence of a forged letter; the celebrated lawyer and spokesman of the Estates, Johann Jakob Moser, for five years on the ground of 'unruly and unbridled behaviour' (i.e. speaking out against the Duke).

In short, for the first half of his reign Karl Eugen enjoyed all the opportunities and fulfilled none of the responsibilities of power. His former patron Frederick the Great, in whose Berlin he had spent the two years before acceding, but without apparently picking up anything of the Prussian King's frugal dedication to duty, wrote that 'the Duke enjoys disorder and seems determined to leave his successors a ruined country'; he had indeed managed to emulate the French monarchy at least in the size of his debts. In 1764, all else failing, the Estates laid a formal list of complaints before the Imperial Council in Vienna, and in 1770 a judgement was passed on all points in their favour, though tactfully disguised under the title 'hereditary settlement'. But just as the Duke's powers were being limited from without, in 1771 he met Franziska von Leutrum who was to be his mistress and eventually wife for the rest of his days, and she achieved his reform from within. So much so that on his fiftieth birthday in February 1778 he had a 'manifesto' read from every pulpit in the land, confessing his past failings, declaring himself born again, and promising in the 'second period of Our life' a new devotion to justice and the welfare of his people.

This is the changed man who in 1771 founded the Academy and spent much of his time overseeing it. There looks to be a satisfying symmetry: half a reign as profligate and despot, then, saved by the love of a good woman, the second half filled with virtue and good works. The pulpit manifesto, too, seems edifying in the manner of a baroque morality play, not to say a parody of moral decision in one of Schiller's own late dramas. But then Karl Eugen had, if nothing else, a taste for theatre—comic theatre, it seemed to Schiller, whose poem 'The Evil Monarchs' (published in 1782) includes these words:

> You pay the debt of youthful bankruptcy
> With vows and virtue laughable to see,
> Inventions of a clown.   (i. 107)

And, motives and sincerity apart, how deep did change go in practice? Württemberg life was not transformed at a stroke. Finances remained shaky, the Duke still went in for extravagant building and entertaining, there was a further 'subsidy' treaty, this time with Holland. Worse, his most infamous act of arbitrary imprisonment fell in the 'reformed' years. In 1777, the poet and journalist Schubart was lured on to Württemberg territory and arrested. He had coined the phrase 'slave plantation' for the Academy, and celebrated its founder's new leanings with an epigram:

> When Dionysius of Syracuse
> Gave up the ways of tyranny,
> What did he choose to be?
> A country dominie.

Schubart was held for ten years, again as in the earlier cases a vindictiveness out of all proportion to the offence. Franziska, apparently, looked on as Schubart was led into the Hohenasperg fortress.

All this suggests more continuity than contrast between the two halves of Karl Eugen's reign. So does the history of the Academy itself. As a 'military seminary' for sons of the nobility and middle classes to be trained for the army and the professions, it dates from 1771. But it was not founded on a sudden new beneficent impulse. Humbler training enterprises preceded it: an academy of arts, a school for the building trades: expensive foreign artists and craftsmen were to be replaced by cheaper local products wholly under the Duke's control. That would ease his financial difficulties. The Academy's purpose was just as practical: to train cadres of unquestioningly loyal public servants, indebted for and indoctrinated by their education. Thus a scheme to lessen the Duke's bills was backed by a scheme to lessen the traditional Württemberg spirit of opposition.

The Academy was run accordingly: the pupils in military uniform, under military discipline and close supervision; no holidays or compassionate leave; rarely visitors. An application to leave the school for good was treated as something between a breach of discipline and a personal affront to the Duke. If granted, it meant repaying the full cost of the education so far received. The Duke's regular visits had to be met with regular obsequiousness towards him and his mistress, particularly in ceremonial addresses of flattery and gratitude which the pupils (Schiller included) had to compose and deliver.

Local historians and apologists for Karl Eugen argue that some of this—uniform, separation from parents—was Enlightenment practice, found in other schools of the period; that Schiller would have been as cramped and constrained in the Tübingen Seminary which his ambition would have preferred; that taking education out of the hands of the Protestant authorities was forward-looking; that many sound men were trained at the Academy who looked back on it with gratitude; and that for anyone but a poet, with it (it is implied) an excessive and unrepresentative 'lust for liberty', this was an undertaking of enlightened modernity.

Yet the 'lust' for liberty is crucial, and no institution that represses it can properly be called 'enlightened'. True Enlightenment, as it was already understood for example in Kant's essays of the 1780s, which sum up the values evolved in Germany over several decades, means giving free scope to the individual's perceptions and potential without laying down a fixed course for their development, in the faith that human variety and its free interaction are ultimately to the public good. Karl Eugen's strictly instrumental use of local abilities was neither enlightened nor, in the true sense, education. It was training. And though Schiller's reaction in his first play, *The Robbers*, goes far beyond the Enlightenment's measured conception of social change, and does so with a violence of action and language that was consciously designed to get the work 'burned by the public hangman', that does not make his frustrated desire for freedom merely eccentric or unrepresentative. The explosive force of words and imagination which makes him exceptional is his way of being, precisely, representative. For what else does the poet's function consist in, if not to voice human experiences and needs where others grope for expression or do not dare to speak?

That freedom was centrally at issue in the Academy was plain even to the casual eye. A young woman visitor in 1783—seven years later she was to become Schiller's wife—wrote that 'the human heart with its innate instinct for liberty has a strange feeling of unease at the sight of these young men assembled for their meal. Each of their movements follows a signal from the supervisor. It is painful to see human creatures treated like puppets.' Schiller's own later image for the inertness that despots require of their subjects goes further: what claimed to be a concern for their education was only a 'fashionable fancy to trade in God's creatures' (the Academy's printed report forms actually referred to the pupils as 'wares'), a 'rage to turn out human beings as Deucalion did—with the difference that he turned stones into men, whereas these turn men into stones' (v. 829). And when Karl Eugen died, Schiller went further still, invoking not Classical myth but the Christian story: 'Old Herod', he wrote, was dead (to Körner, 10 Dec. 1793). Not then just a manipulator of men, but a slaughterer of innocence, the loss of which is one of Schiller's deepest themes.

Schiller's youthful trauma was vital to the genesis of his early works and is vital to our assessment of them. A would-be dramatist might have seen how absolutism operated by studying Württemberg history, or from a detached observation of Karl Eugen's (or almost any other petty German prince's) reign. But Schiller's early experience made absolutism a felt reality, continuing into his own day, reaching into his own life. It drove him to rebel by the only means available, the pen. He conducted a guerrilla warfare between the lines of the dutiful reports and those grovelling ceremonial speeches the system required; he wrote sardonic and satirical poems, as well as passionate and philosophical ones, and dedicated the collection—*Anthology for 1782*—with macabre medical honesty to 'my Principal, Death' (i. 29); he burst into open protest with *The Robbers*; he mounted a seemingly lurid yet substantially accurate indictment of small-state despotism in the domestic tragedy *Intrigue and Love*; and in *Don Carlos*, going far beyond the local scene but still drawing on it in spirit and psychological detail, he set an impassioned statement of liberal principles against the legendary tyranny of Philip II of Spain and the Inquisition.

All of which, if we allowed Karl Eugen and his regime to be made out as harmlessly 'modern' and enlightened, would seem mere self-induced melodrama, the internal overheating of young genius before it really knows what the world is about, and at best a feverish prelude to the mature works of an imagination that was later to engage soberly with the processes of history. But in truth Schiller's early works are the first phase of that engagement. History began in the present; to feel its forces pressing in and threatening to crush him was, grimly enough, a gift for the dramatist. It was an education in and by absolutism.

'Commerce of mind and body'

The study of medicine decisively formed Schiller's imagination and theoretical outlook. He took it up in 1776 with no great enthusiasm, but at least it would liberate him from law, which was an arid world for an aspiring poet, and it did bear on recognizably the same complex and suffering humanity that literature was concerned with. More directly so, indeed, than it does now. With pharmacology and surgery still primitive, much medicine involved observing and speculating on how mind and body interacted, and how the ills of the one might be cured by treating the other. It thus contained the raw material for a dramatist's applied psychology. It was also close to philosophy— Schiller's favourite among the general subjects taught in the Academy—one of whose central problems, at least since Descartes, had been the 'commerce of mind and body'. This was to remain Schiller's central question, and his response never loses touch with its origins in his medical training. Faced with problems of culture, ethics, or politics, his essays are prescriptions for restoring health, shrewd dosings with the compensatory elements the case requires.

The question still unanswered in the late eighteenth century was how two such disparate things as mind and body, a 'thinking substance' and an 'extended substance', could connect at all. It is true there were some standard models: the link between mind and body was part of the universal harmony pre-established by God, they were like two clocks, unconnected but synchronized at the start once for all (Leibniz); or the divine intervention was repeated on each separate occasion when a mental act appeared to cause a bodily movement, or when action upon the body appeared to cause a mental event (the 'occasionalism' of the Dutch Cartesian Geulincx). But these were not so much explanations as evasions. Medical theorists wanted instead a model of the mutual influence of body and mind which did not call in the deity. Yet on the accepted definitions of what body and mind were, any real influence must mean that at the point of contact body was somehow spiritual in nature, or mind was somehow material. How else could either get a purchase on the other? Bridging the gap between the traditional entities meant abolishing the distinct nature of one of them.

The question was, which should go? It was hard to see how the body could in the last analysis be ethereal, and such an assumption went against the ever more marked empiricist grain of the day. Even a theory that 'soul' was a governing principle without which there could be no coherent organism at all (the 'animism' of Georg Ernst Stahl), though it distantly echoed Aristotle and may now seem a forerunner of psychosomatic and therapeutic approaches, in its time looked more like mysticism, a failure to escape from religious notions. At the other extreme, materialist explanations of mind invited attack from a still powerful religious orthodoxy: they dissolved the soul into mechanistic workings and replaced free will with physical determinism, which tarred them with the brush of the scandalous French atheism allegedly to be found in La Mettrie's *L'Homme machine* (1748).

So perhaps it was better to live with uncertainty and give up speculating altogether. The Swiss physiologist and poet Albrecht von Haller praised the modesty of those who admitted ignorance of exactly how the Creator had linked mind and body and stuck instead to the laws experience revealed. Simply asserting the reality of our dual nature, however imperfectly understood, and keeping a balance between the elements, became the stated goal of a new science, 'andrology' or 'anthropology'. The proper study of mankind was the whole man. Even so, since mind as such is by definition not observable, an apparent resignation like Haller's tended to settle the old controversy one way: 'spiritual' explanations had largely depended on speculation, and an empirical approach necessarily edged towards materialism.

These problems and positions are plainly visible in Schiller's medical writings. His essay *Philosophy of Physiology*, of which only part survives, states the familiar question and riffles through the familiar pseudo-solutions before offering his own. This is a 'medial force' (*Mittelkraft*, or in the original Latin *vis transmutatoria*) which makes the desired connection between physical sensation and mental world (v. 253). He locates this force in an 'infinitely subtle' entity he calls 'nerve-spirit' which dwells in the nerve canals. Its combination of one physical component('nerve') and one non-physical ('spirit') is designed to make communication between mental and physical worlds plausible, but it only shifts the problem back one stage: for how do the components of the hybrid manage to combine? The same applies to the other concepts that then fall thick and fast—'material idea', 'sensuous spirits', 'material thinking', all somehow contrived by the 'medial force'. The workings of the whole system are put down to an 'eternal law' (v. 256), so that we seem to be back at pre-established harmony. Can Schiller be serious? He has begun by saying that a force partaking of both material and spiritual qualities is strictly inconceivable. Yet he now brushes that objection firmly aside: 'Experience proves it. How can theory reject it?' (v. 254). Body and mind, 'material nature' and 'active soul', are licensed to act upon each other because we know they actually do. He has cut the Gordian knot —or perhaps rather joined together the Gordian loose ends.

None of this can have altogether surprised Schiller's examiners (it was his passing-out thesis for the Academy). Haller had already talked of nerve-spirit, and others, cautiously, of a possible intermediary force, although no one had put them forward together, or with this forthrightness. But Schiller was failed. His style was 'too flowery', some of his philosophical arguments 'difficult', and above all he had shown a 'dangerous tendency to know better'. He had criticized 'the worthiest men', even 'the immortal Haller'. An illiberal spirit speaks through these comments. Final decisions were left to the Duke, himself an admirer of Haller. He decided that Schiller had shown 'mettle' but written 'too ardently', he would benefit from another year in the Academy 'where his fire may be a little dampened'.

This minute episode in the history of medicine is more

significant as an episode in Schiller's relations with authority. Being a not exceptionally keen student, but—despite the Academy's regime—an irrepressibly independent mind, with a strong interest in psychology, he had composed a bold dissertation, taking his subject by the scruff of the neck and giving it (he hoped) a final good shake so as to get out of these walls. His essay is as much self-assertion as investigation. Precisely these qualities provoked authority to put him in his place.

There was no taking chances second time round. Schiller wrote two further dissertations, belt-and-braces: one on a concrete question in pathology, the classification of fevers, and one more wide-ranging, *On the Connection between Man's Animal and Spiritual Natures*—the same theme as in *Philosophy of Physiology*, but to be treated (so he promised when he submitted the subject, no doubt with the criticisms of his 'difficult' philosophical arguments in mind) 'very physiologically' (v. 324).

Still, his independence had not evaporated. The preface argues for the Hippocratic art as a philosophical discipline, not just a mechanical livelihood. It also, on a different level, reminds Karl Eugen frankly of those 'most favourable prospects' he had promised years before to the boy who wanted to be a preacher (v. 288). This dissertation also has a clearer personal emphasis than its predecessor, which kept the familiar options of materialism and idealism open. Though Schiller declares himself opposed to extremes, he is noticeably harder on the idealist rejection of our physical nature, which arises so readily from the Christian tradition. He commits himself to showing 'the remarkable contribution of the body to the actions of the soul, and the great and real influence of animal sensation on things spiritual' (v. 290 f.). Despite the impermanence of things physical, and the moral necessity of sometimes struggling against bodily impulse, which makes human beings (in a phrase he takes from Haller) 'miserable mixtures of beast and angel' (v. 296), still it is sensation and physical need that stimulate the individual and the race to new advances, to the devising of everything from skills and cities via gods to Newtonian science. 'The body is the first spur to action, sensuous existence the first ladder to perfection' (v. 306).

Which is not to deny important reverse influences of mind on body. He instances the curative effect of joy; or the undermining effect of mental torment (he illustrates this from literature—a mysterious 'Life of Moor. Tragedy by Krake' which is his own *Robbers* in disguise); or even the permanent shaping of the human features by habitual emotions ('The further the mind strays from the image of God, the nearer does the external form come to the beast'—v. 317).

All this does not keep Schiller's promise to treat his theme 'very physiologically', at least not in any precise empirical way. He admits that to prove his propositions from hospital practice would be an endless task. His essay on fevers too was empirical only at second hand. His only first-hand observations that survive are some reports on a fellow student, Grammont, who suffered from acute melancholia; and here problems of diagnosis and treatment are hard to distinguish from the protest—of doctor as well as patient—against the institutional confinement that had brought on the illness. Schiller took the gentle approach, gained the sufferer's confidence by seeing his point of view, and thereby lost the confidence of the authorities. Grammont, predictably, recovered completely when released from the Academy.

Schiller's own attempt to secure his release succeeded this time, though his examiners did criticize his main dissertation for its materialist emphasis. One of them however was in good measure responsible for it: Schiller's philosophy teacher Jakob Friedrich Abel, who—appropriately for his subject—did more than anyone to let some light of liberality into the Academy's intended utilitarian training. Abel's classes included open-minded discussion of notorious materialist thinkers like La Mettrie and Helvétius; and indeed his own published work, for example the *Speech on Genius* of 1776 from which Schiller drew inspiration, argues much the same dependence of mental operations on bodily sensation that Schiller's essay does. Examining Schiller, he could see his own views reflected perhaps a little too directly. In fact, this close relation to a much-loved teacher turns what may look like a complex problem in intellectual history into a pedagogical truism. For the many medical and philosophical authorities quoted or implied in Schiller's early writings did not all come at him separately and in the original, to be synthesized by the light of his own judgement. They must have been predigested and presented largely by Abel. Schiller's dissertations owe their grand overview and their (over-)confidence to his teacher. They mark that final stage of dependent independence before a pupil's vigorous mind moves off on its own paths.

The broader framework of these early essays is the common eighteenth-century question: how can Man achieve his destined perfection in the real world? Both their medical orientation and the pressures of the institution he was writing in prevented Schiller from discussing social factors. But his interest in them was certainly alive. Abel records how his pupils would meet him at the gates and talk him all the way to the classroom, then back again afterwards. They talked philosophical shop, personal affairs, and politics. Sometimes this peripatetic prelude extended some way into the lesson itself, 'not to the disadvantage of the students'. Given a liberal inch, they took a yard—it is hard to keep education within functional bounds, once it is fostered at all. Philosophy, physiology, medicine, politics, the personal life: in the end they all made up the one discipline of human nature and its proper health and ends, a vital discipline when there was so much in society to damage and impede them.

And a young doctor was supposed to be able to cure. But all Schiller was asked to cure after qualifying was the ills of Augé's Grenadiers, a run-down regiment of invalids and veterans. His pay for this uninspiring job was 216 gulden a year (for comparison, a professor earned around a thousand, Karl Eugen's opera singers as much as five thousand). These were the long-promised brilliant prospects. But Schiller's mind was already running on larger remedies.

Theatrical sensation

'What medicines will not cure, iron will cure; what iron will not cure, fire will cure.' Hippocrates, father of medicine, was stating the sequence of increasingly drastic treatments—medication, the knife, cauterization—which the necessity of the case might lead a doctor to use. The words have a grimmer glint when they stand as epigraph to a drama of vengeful violence. Karl Moor in *The Robbers* (*Die Räuber*, 1782) puts men to the sword and burns a town in the course of his rebellion. But what is he, and behind him Schiller, out to cure? Surely the evils of absolute power: this is Schiller's legendary first outburst after years of constraint, the product (he said later) of 'the unnatural intercourse of genius and oppression' (v. 855). The issues seem clear: freedom versus tyranny. It should be a work not just of released energy but of heroic simplicity. Yet it is not so straightforward; and precisely its inner tensions and contradictions make the young Schiller himself an interesting case, a writer who has, or is caught in, a nexus of more resistant and permanently important themes.

Karl Moor finds ample injustice and corruption to avenge, much of it typical of the absolutist order; his band is feared by tyrants and joined by their victims. But what first drives him to become an outlaw is not social protest but private injury. His father casts him out just when he has resolved to leave behind his student life of debts and debauch. When the 'Prodigal Son' (a title Schiller considered for the stage version) is refused forgiveness, his good nature turns instantly into 'universal hatred'. He agrees to lead his admiring friends in robbery, provided they will murder too. The violence seems disproportionate and indiscriminate. Even the father–son conflict, which it might be argued Schiller is using as a symbol for social protest, has been engineered by Karl's wicked brother Franz (like Edmund in *King Lear*, Franz has 'a credulous father, and a brother noble' on whose 'foolish honesty [his] practices ride easy'). So the underlying reality is a conflict between brothers, which is not as apt to carry that symbolic social meaning.

Still, for three acts Karl's tragic illusion that his mild and loving father has disinherited him fuels what amounts to open war on a not very clearly defined authority. Perhaps the initial motive matters less than the result? Yet the conduct of that war is not presented simply either. Karl, after the blood-lust of his first reaction, becomes a 'noble' outlaw, a 'sublime criminal' of the kind Rousseau pointed to in Plutarch's biographies of the great Greeks and Romans (i. 622). He is a Robin Hood (i. 565) who punishes the wicked and leaves plunder to the others. But those others are the problem. His noble ends are belied and betrayed by his band. Apart from the one virtue of loyalty to him, they are brutal and callous. His daring rescue of a comrade from the gallows is soured by their gratuitous murder of women and children. 'How this deed weighs on me! It has poisoned my finest works.' Destruction for its own sake is not after all what he wanted. It casts doubt on his whole enterprise. He can no longer believe in himself as 'the man to wield the avenging sword of the higher tribunals' (i. 548).

This is a scruple that might not have been expected from a wild hero or from his rebellious author. Yet the questioning and retractation of violence structure the entire play. Karl is first seen railing against the 'limp age of eunuchs' he lives in, and aspiring to amoral greatness at any price: 'Give me an army of fellows like me, and Germany shall become a republic that will make Rome and Sparta look like nunneries' (i. 504). But the Prodigal has already taken the decision to return home, so that his challenge to the social conventions which have 'ruined the flight of eagles and turned it into the creeping of snails' is undone in advance. Later there is his revulsion at the violence committed by his wholly unidealistic followers. And the drama ends with Karl's surrender to the forces of order. He has by now returned home, impelled by yearning though well aware that his crimes preclude a full moral return and a happy ending. With father and brother dead, and finally his fiancée sacrificed by his own hand to purge the oath he took never to abandon his men, he gives himself up to expiate the 'foolish' belief that he could 'make the world beautiful through atrocities and uphold the laws through lawlessness'. He realizes that 'two men like me would bring down the whole structure of the moral world.' He is not addressing mere secular authority, which can be reinstated at this point the more easily for never having been fully portrayed. but the divine order behind it: 'Mercy—mercy for the boy who tried to do Thy work—vengeance is Thine alone' (i. 617).

The religious turn is surprising till we recall Schiller's early leanings and the traditional piety of seventeenth- and eighteenth-century Swabia whose influence he cannot have escaped. But the vital concession is in the word 'boy'. It gainsays the Enlightenment's central insistence on an adult mankind that would think and act for itself, independently of father-figures and self-appointed guardians. Such action now appears as childish error, and the repenting rebel son hands back all responsibility to the ultimate father. There are further recantations to come, too. Schiller was to write an anonymous review of his own play, sharp enough to be attacked by another critic for being too severe; and as if his hero had not made amends enough at the close, he planned a sequel that would be 'an entire apologia of the author for the first part' (to Dalberg, 24 Aug. 1784).

The play's contradictions have puzzled many readers. The easy solution is to say, with Carlyle, that its power makes up for its inconsistencies; or to enjoy the strange blend of rebellion with remorse, and the melancholy poetic broodings on human imperfection and the lost Elysium of innocent childhood (i. 561 f. and 569), as the Romantic mystery of a prototype Byronic hero. But the paradox of activism and self-doubt is not a mere literary effect. It gives artistic form to a basic psychological and political question, namely, how can a flawed humanity put ideals into practice? How can it distinguish legitimate ideals from the mere impulse to act out violent fantasies? And even if rebellion appears legitimate, how can the measures it demands be themselves kept within moral bounds? Before the century was out, the French Revolution was to pose all these questions in its own dramatic way. The tragic saturnalia of Schiller's first drama enacts the issues in advance with unconscious prescience. (Literature does not always wait to reflect, passively, the processes of history.)

The Robbers also hints at lines of thought he was to pursue in the mid-nineties in response to the violent events in France. The brothers are fundamentally different human types, head and heart both taken to fateful extremes. Karl acts from emotion and repents from emotion; though his impulses are at root good, aimed at restoring values like justice and humaneness, he swings unstably from hasty action to a paralysing regret. Brother Franz is cold and calculating, an out-and-out materialist who denies all moral categories and 'natural' emotions. Nature has made him grotesquely ugly, custom provides no inheritance for second sons. Why should he love his more favoured brother, or the father who has always doted on Karl? It would only hinder his ruthless self-interest, in pursuit of which he uses nature's one compensating gift, ingenuity. He plots to discredit Karl and to kill their father by the shock effect of false reports—a malevolent application of the medical theory of mind–body influence. Franz is, in short, what the Enlightenment and its critics feared: the free-thinker who dissolves the constraints of a Christian society altogether, instead of reaffirming them but with a new, secular motivation. Schiller in his own review of the play is duly disturbed to find arguments for Franz's 'vicious system' arising from 'enlightened thinking and liberal study', as well as to find such extreme ideas put so unhesitatingly into practice (i. 626 f.).

The unbalanced rebellions of both brothers fail. Franz commits suicide when guilty nightmares and the arguments of the local pastor shake his atheistic self-assurance. Less plausibly than with the sensitive Karl (but then Franz is a more profoundly subversive figure, who must somehow be made to fail and be seen to fail) religion is what undermines his radical individualism. That symbolizes the grip of convention on minds as well as on social structures. What these structures are, Schiller's play does not show in full. But it does recognize the authority of a *status quo* which the noble robber's onslaught has left intact in all its imperfection. It seems that, in the concluding words of Hippocrates' aphorism which Schiller omitted from his epigraph to *The Robbers*, 'what fire will not cure must definitely be considered incurable'.

The play that reached the Mannheim stage in January 1782 was not quite the original text. The administrator Freiherr von Dalberg, chary of even so much contemporary reference as the play contained, tried to tone it down. He enforced a shift of scene to the early sixteenth century and a number of other changes for the milder which Schiller was in no position to refuse—all this on top of Karl's inner division and his retracting of revolt, which were central to Schiller's conception. Even so the première was a sensation. Pre-publication of the text drew a large audience and their reactions were extraordinary: 'The theatre was like a madhouse: rolling eyeballs, clenched fists, stamping feet, hoarse cries in the auditorium! Complete strangers fell sobbing into each other's arms, women staggered almost fainting to the door. It was a general state of dissolution, like a chaos from whose mists a new creation is breaking forth.'

These excesses match the play itself at its wildest, indeed they read like an extended sample of Schiller's own stage-directions. Sensational *The Robbers* has remained ever since, irresistible whenever performed and credited in popular legend with a direct revolutionary message. Perhaps contemporary audiences ignored the sixteenth-century setting Dalberg had imposed, and pieced together a picture of their own times from the scattered references to absolutist abuses. Certainly the feel of the play is not archaic and detached, it has a wild immediacy. Later it seemed relevant, whether to Schiller himself or some-one else is not clear, to embellish the title-page of the second edition with the words 'In tirannos' (against the tyrants)—a historic phrase the Reformer Ulrich von Hutten had flung at an earlier Duke of Württemberg. And in 1792 the French Revolutionary leaders thought it right to make Schiller an honorary French citizen on the grounds of their 'similar' political situation. Politically committed producers have gone on reviving the play for its revolutionary impact (though Erwin Piscator's famous 1926 production showed up that divided mind of Karl Moor's as a 'bourgeois weakness'). Even today the controversial dramatist Rolf Hochhuth sees in *The Robbers* an archetypal and ever-necessary protest by the 'absolutism of youth'. It is as if the playwright's rebellious intentions and gestures, both physical and verbal, made—and can still make—intuitive contact with audiences, bypassing those elements of his text which take back rebellion; as if violence once uttered or enacted on stage cannot wholly *be* taken back, or at any rate not by such dramatically weaker means as remorse and a return to the fold of morality late in the action. Karl's self-doubt and contrition, and even his final grand gesture of self-sacrifice, are no match for his wilder words and deeds. These may seem overdone, Gothic, grand guignol. Coleridge labelled them 'the material sublime'— 'to produce an effect, he sets you a whole town on fire . . . But Shakespeare drops a handkerchief, and the same or greater effect follows.' Yet Coleridge himself, when young, was carried away by the first drama of this 'bard tremendous in sublimity'. And Schiller's obvious sublime effects are not the whole story. They are backed by a skilful manipulation of our natural sympathy for outcasts which operates through a network of allusions to the heroic rebels and outsiders of literature—Milton's Satan, Shakespeare's Brutus, and (implicitly) the two figures with whom the young Goethe, the 'god' of young literary enthusiasts at the Academy, had made a European reputation within the last decade: Karl Moor combines the fighting prowess of Goethe's medieval knight Götz von Berlichingen and the reflective sensitivities of his Werther. Just as compellingly in the creation of antipathy, the cynical and misshapen Franz calls to mind Iago and Richard III. All this, together with a deft handling of scenic and thematic contrast, makes Schiller already in his first play a master of the larger language of theatre. 'If we are ever to expect a German Shakespeare', a prophetic reviewer wrote, 'this is the man.'

Yet if we are to believe Schiller's foreword to *The Robbers*, he was not sure of being 'theatrical' at all. He claims he did not have stage performance in view, but used the dramatic mode as a means to 'catch the mind in its most secret operations' (i. 484). Franz, the 'reasoning villain', was meant for the 'thinking reader' to take from the page rather than for the action-loving spectator to see in action (to Dalberg, 6 Oct. 1781). Some of this may be coquetry or precautionary sour grapes—any untried dramatic author must wonder whether his dreams will ever come true in the theatre. But it was also genuine doubt about how much psychological intricacy could be conveyed on stage. Two generations of German critics and dramatists had questioned long-accepted valuations and assumptions. Not only had the allegedly Aristotelean unities been flouted and the supremacy of French classical tragedy with all its elaborate conventions denied, the primacy of drama itself was under question. Germans were beginning to recognize the immense potential of the novel as a means to come at modern life and modern sensibility, they were striving to emulate Fielding's range and Sterne's subtlety. So when Schiller speaks of his 'dramatic novel' (i. 482) he is implicitly drawing *The Robbers* away from the old-established theatrical genre. But this is where the

23

Mannheim premiere was decisive. It showed him what could still be done in the theatre, and proved to him—in case he had really doubted it—where his power and genius lay. Even Franz uses a rhetoric that demands to be spoken, and not (as the novel is by its readers) 'self-administered in private'. In language as in gesture, Schiller's was an essentially public talent, needing a public space in which to unfold and have its full effect. The aspiring provincial, well aware that he had never before seen any but 'mediocre' stage presentation, could now say: 'If Germany is one day to find in me a dramatic poet, the beginnings date from last week's performance' (to Dalberg, 25 Dec. 1781, 17 Jan. 1782).

The full implications of that sensational evening's theatre were not yet clear and still had to emerge from those 'mists of chaos'. They did so over the next two years, and were then declared in a public statement on the power of theatrical sensation which is also the first of Schiller's grand utterances on what art means to society. This too was before a Mannheim audience.

Flight

For the second decisive consequence of the Mannheim production was Schiller's flight from Stuttgart. It had been bad enough to go back to his humdrum post after the excitement of being a fêted author, and he begged Dalberg—unsuccessfully—to intercede with the Duke and get permission for him to work in Mannheim. But then complaints came in from the Swiss canton which Schiller's text had branded a rogues' paradise (i. 538) while the Duke also learned that his regimental doctor had gone absent without leave to attend a further performance of his play. Schiller suffered a fortnight's arrest and a ban henceforth on any but medical writing. He appealed on the grounds that he needed the extra income his creative writing provided, and felt an obligation to his own talent. The Duke refused to listen and forbade further appeals on pain of punishment. Once again he was an absolute obstacle to Schiller's ambition. This ban on the one thing Schiller aspired to do, and now knew he could do, left him little choice. On 22 September 1782, accompanied by his musician friend Andreas Streicher who wanted to study with

C.P.E. Bach in Hamburg, he absconded. The escape had some nicely characteristic features. Despite the tension of the appointed day, Schiller wrote a new poem and made Streicher comment on it before they left. Meanwhile Duke Karl Eugen was entertaining the Russian Grand Duke Paul and his wife and hundred-and-one retinue (cost: 345,000 gulden) and as the fugitives drove out of Stuttgart into the night they had at their backs the hubbub and fireworks of one more lavish festivity. In a nearby wood six thousand deer from all over Württemberg waited hemmed in by all-night fires, to be slaughtered *en masse* the next day by the noble party.

In breaking out, Schiller was following and trusting in his genius. His teacher Abel's speech *On Genius* had drawn a poetic contrast between the cautious and conformist 'creeping of snails' and the legendary flight of the eagle to the sun in search of self-renewal. Schiller had borrowed those images for his Karl Moor, and now dramatically taken flight himself. But he had no firm prospects and could only look to Dalberg for help. Dalberg was slow to respond, and Schiller was left in every way insecure. He lacked openings to live by his pen, or even to practise medicine in Mannheim. He feared reprisals against his family, he feared (with the kidnap of Schubart in mind) for himself, he tried to stay incognito, shifted addresses, wrote misleading letters. Poetic rhetoric apart, it was not certain whether this was the triumphant flight of an eagle or the flight of an Icarus who had striven too high and was now falling.

Intrigues

Schiller brought with him to Mannheim his second play, *The Conspiracy of Fiesco at Genoa (Die Verschwörung des Fiesco zu Genua*, 1783). Dalberg had encouraged the plan but now rejected the finished work, refusing even an *ex gratia* payment for the labour Schiller had put in. He was obviously embarrassed by this fugitive from a neighbouring territory (he had just been to the grand Russian reception himself). Only when it seemed sure that the Duke of Württemberg had accepted Schiller's desertion as an accomplished fact—and when the Mannheim theatre found itself seriously short of good plays—did Dalberg renew contact with Schiller, who had by then survived a year on loans and charity. He gave him a year's contract as Mannheim theatre-poet at a salary of three hundred gulden, hardly more than Schiller's old medical pittance, plus one or two benefit performances: not very generous for a writer whose first play had already made him a household name. Schiller meantime had been working without complaint—this, after all, was 'freedom'—had adapted *Fiesco* and written *Louisa Miller*, later renamed *Intrigue and Love*. Both plays treat political and social themes: a sixteenth-century revolt against tyranny, and the breaking up of a love-affair across the boundaries of class by a ruthless court cabal. Both also aspire to be tragedy.

The relatively obscure figure of Fiesco came on Rousseau's recommendation, as a modern whose rebellion in 1547 against the tyrant of Genoa, Andrea Doria, set him on a par with the great Greeks and Romans celebrated in Plutarch's biographies. He was 'brought up to free his homeland from the rule of the Dorias . . . there was no other thought in his mind but to overthrow the usurper'. But Schiller's Fiesco is no more straightforward than his Karl Moor. Where the robbers' leader acted and repented, Fiesco is undecided how to act. Admired and charismatic but devious, he hides his plan of revolt behind a mask of Epicurean high living, and his deepest intentions are obscure. When he eventually shows his hand to the members of an existing conspiracy (to that extent the play's title is misleading) he demands to be its 'sovereign' (i. 707 f.). The word sounds ominous in good republican ears. Is Fiesco moved by public spirit or personal ambition? He himself has yet to resolve that question. Looking out over the city, he muses that 'to win a crown is to be great, to cast it aside is divine'; and he resolves to free Genoa and be its 'happiest citizen' (i. 659). But two scenes later he has changed his ideas: 'Virtue? The sublime mind has other temptations than the common—does it really have to share the same virtue? Must the armour that constrains a pygmy's form also fit the body of a giant?' (i. 698). And yet another, more radical option than the choice between power-seeking or republicanism is added when Fiesco's wife Leonore begs him to renounce the dehumanizing world of politics altogether and escape with her to the 'romantic scenes' of a

Rousseauian Elysium (i. 731 f.). What shall it profit a man if he gain power but lose his full humanity? (He first loses her, incidentally, killed by his own hand when she joins the street fighting in male disguise.)

The outcome stays uncertain till the very end, when Fiesco, despite Shakespearean echoes in the text which seem to cast him as Brutus, does indeed seize power for himself and is duly killed by the true republican Verrina. But even this does not settle matters finally, because Fiesco's problem is also his author's. Schiller could not decide what his hero's real nature was to be under the onion-skins of dissimulation and wavering. He changed the pattern just described (the published text) in a stage version eventually put on in Mannheim, ending it with virtue triumphant and a 'happiest citizen' curtain-line borrowed from the earlier scene, while yet another stage version, for Leipzig, went back to Fiesco-the-tyrant, only killing him off by slightly different means (i. 952,965). It looks rather as if Schiller was experimenting with diametrically opposed kinds of greatness, the 'immoralist' kind that presumes to rise above ordinary restraints in some grand deed, or the moral kind that recreates restraint from within in an act of 'self-overcoming' (i. 753). He was experimenting, that is, to see which would be dramatically the more effective of these two forms of self-assertion. (Schiller's psychological understanding of their interrelation strikingly anticipates Nietzsche's analysis of the Will to Power.)

This seems prime evidence for an iconoclastic view of Schiller dating from the 1960s, namely that far from being the dramatic moralist he has always been thought, he was only ever out for effect at any price. It is certainly true that Schiller's stagecraft is never far from the *coup de théâtre*, and in the playbill text for *Fiesco* he plainly relishes the 'great moment' when he has the audience's souls 'on a lead', or can 'toss them like a ball towards heaven or hell' (i. 754). But just as plainly his effects are designed for a moral purpose. He worried over how much could be picked up in performance by an audience, as distinct from the reader who can 'disentangle even the most confused thread' (i. 753). He wanted both to complicate things for the printed text and simplify things for the stage (to Dalberg, 16 Nov. 1782).

27

And when it came to deciding on a stage-ending, he was torn precisely for reasons of moral effectiveness between letting his audience learn a lesson from the sight of a criminal being punished, or making them 'vie with a [morally] great man' (i. 753). Leipzig audiences got the first, Mannheim audiences the second and perhaps less conventional solution, the one that draws them into participating actively in a psychological and moral process that stretches beyond the play, rather than passively receiving a familiar doctrine that concludes it. This is already typical of Schiller's dynamic aesthetics.

Yet whether we talk of page or stage, and of this or that ending, Schiller was once more probing a vital political question. Will the personal ambition of exceptional beings serve the public good? Can those who have the energy to act and lead also have the maturity and generosity to pass up power for themselves? Is today's liberator not almost bound to be tomorrow's new tyrant? Or can the welfare of other human beings give him a satisfaction that will outweigh the pleasure of dominating? Once again a seemingly straightforward revolt has been complicated by the individual's morality and motivation. And once again a religious framework is established for these issues at the close, more suggestively this time than at the close of *The Robbers*. Karl Moor simply threw that play awkwardly into reverse with his sudden repentance and submission to the divine as well as the temporal order. Verrina, on the other hand, faced with Fiesco's betrayal of the republican faith, opens up a perspective on political evil which is wholly consistent with this play's intellectual direction. To Fiesco he says: 'I hate you as I hate the serpent in Paradise that brought the first false act into the Creation, from which mankind has been bleeding for these four millennia and more' (i. 749). Betrayal of the good has a long tradition, and the power of original sin might seem almost an excuse for modern evil. But in hating Fiesco as much as its mythic originator, Verrina is giving him an equal responsibility. It is as if Fiesco has re-enacted the corruption of Man. Each new failure of political integrity or idealism dashes human hopes for a fresh start, each is a new Fall, another tragedy of lost innocence. Republicanism, Rousseauism, Christianity are related value-systems that take strength from each other's concepts and rhetoric. They all hark back to a pristine state and they all look forward to a time when it will be restored. Meanwhile politics and society are the fallen condition, the vale of tears.

Innocence and the serpent, purity and politics, again shape the conflict in *Intrigue and Love* (*Kabale und Liebe*, 1784). This time the innocent are not corrupted but deceived and out-manœuvred by the cynical. The idealistic Ferdinand, son of a ruthless First Minister (like Karl Eugen's Montmartin) in a small state, finds love in a bourgeois 'house of innocence' (i. 794). He sets the absolute claims of 'heaven's handwriting in Louisa's eyes' against the conventions of the social hierarchy, and in particular against his father's plan to marry him off to the ruler's mistress for the sake of political influence, while the ruler makes a marriage of dynastic convenience elsewhere. Ferdinand proposes eloping to a Rousseauian wilderness, but Louisa in her stolid attachment to bourgeois religious and family values cannot agree to such an abstract solution. The court's plan to destroy young love relies paradoxically on just this class ethic and on Ferdinand's inability to allow for it: Louisa takes and keeps an oath not to reveal how she was black-mailed into writing the letter which incriminates her in her jealous lover's eyes. Innocence is no match for the calculations of the Minister's adviser, the transparently named Wurm (i.e. the serpent again); it actually undoes itself through its own integrity. Ferdinand's jealousy, already aroused by Louisa's refusal to elope, is quick to believe the false letter. To the pure, all things are suddenly impure: he is faced with the seeming contradiction of 'a heavenly exterior and a devilish heart' in the girl he loved (i. 817). Despair and fury drive him to murder her; his mistake discovered, he kills himself. His father the Minis-ter, ultimately responsible for the tragedy, curses the 'serpent's advice' that has brought it about (i. 857).

Schiller's characters and situations are extreme, and the play is sometimes dismissed as implausible melodrama. Implausib-ilities it does have: an unmasking of the whole intrigue hangs at one point by the thread of a single ambiguous word, which the obsessed Ferdinand misunderstands (i. 821). His jealousy is itself sometimes declared implausible in its extremity, given his earlier feelings. Yet jealousy is by definition extreme, the coextensive shadow of previous love—and is Othello 'plausible'? Equally extreme, and as often criticized, is the sustained high rhetoric of the prose dialogue which mixes strangely with the genre of 'bourgeois tragedy' Schiller was consciously using. (No bourgeois girl ever talked like Louisa.) This was a genuine mismatch of temperament and mode. But what is not implausible, extreme as it too may seem, is the social reality the action grows out of: the oppressive atmosphere, the ruthless machinations, the selling of soldiers for foreign wars, the social and ethical distance between the classes, the political background, the impossibility of redress. What may seem melodramatically exaggerated is built up piece by piece from Schiller's knowledge of Württemberg—including, as mitigation, the portrait (based on Karl Eugen's Franziska) of a ruler's mistress who has tried to place herself between the Prince and his land as between the tiger and the lamb (i. 787). To capture all this, only the extreme was adequate. And the verbal rhetoric is forced to rise to match the events and emotions; only a more mature artist could have managed such a subject by the eloquence of understatement. But the elevated language—which does also have its own stylistic coherence and grandeur—is no reason for disbelieving the substance, as some have done. To mistrust Schiller's picture as too bad to be true, merely because his rhetoric carries him and his characters away, would be to turn deaf ears to a voice that rendered at least poetic justice to generations of silent sufferers.

Not quite a unique voice, it is true. Criticism of courts as 'hells' of moral corruption had a tradition stretching back at least to the Renaissance; and in German hands the new 'bourgeois tragedy', developed in mid-century out of English models and Diderot's innovations in France, had quickly focused on the social and political ills that pressed on the German middle-classes under absolutist rulers. Lessing's *Emilia Galotti* (1772) used themes of seduction, abduction, murder and suicide to indict a system which puts all power in the hands of one man, necessarily unpredictable because 'only human', and abetted in his passions by an unscrupulous underling. The final pathos of the Prince's helpless regret, and the vehemence with which he rejects his Chamberlain, do nothing to diminish the ultimate responsibility of the ruler. Lessing carefully sets his action at a distance, in an imagined Italian principality of Dorsalo—overtly nowhere in Germany, but potentially and essentially anywhere. That was already near the knuckle. Schiller came nearer yet, setting his play 'at the court of a German prince' and packing it with detail that was both documentarily true of Württemberg and par for the petty states generally. The play is not just satire; but like all good satire it is specific when it indicts, giving evil a scarcely veiled local habitation and an implied name. Unlike Lessing, Schiller does not bring the ruler himself on to the stage; but the odour of his reputation reaches and disgusts us—Louisa dare not appeal to the Prince lest she appeal to him too much (i. 813 f.)—and his absence is eloquent through its effects: it leaves the politicians a free hand to destroy innocent people. The accusation is at least as strong as could have been mounted by making the Prince a character in the action.

Schiller warned Dalberg that the play was satirical (3 April 1783). Inevitably, Dalberg ordered cuts for the stage première, notably the scene where the Duke's mistress hears from a servant a graphic account of how local men said farewell to their families and were marched away, hired out by their ruler to fight against the rebellious colonists in America: not just local criticism, but a provocative reminder that a related greater struggle is going on in the background of a smaller. But piecemeal censorship could not tone down a play whose whole conception was social protest.

This is not to say Schiller was interested in nothing else: social protest was not his intended career, literature was. Yet he could not easily keep them apart. Even the final tragic consummation in *Intrigue and Love* barely distracts him from the political theme. His last scene focuses even more intensively than Lessing's had done on the question of responsibility for the death of his lovers. It is of course a rhetorical question, sprung from a vision of Germany as profoundly divided between power and helplessness, pomp and misery, its grandiose pretence of vitality concealing a fundamental sickness. The grim picture is put most strongly in a seldom noted passage of a minor work, an essay of 1785 on the famous Mannheim collection of classical statuary. Writing in the persona of a Danish traveller, Schiller

31

opens with a summary of what he knows southern Germany essentially to be:

> I have seen perhaps the highpoint of splendour and riches. The triumph of human hand over the stubborn resistance of nature often astonished me—but the misery dwelling nearby soon infected my pleasurable wonderment. A hollow-eyed figure of hunger that begs from me in the flowery avenues of a princely pleasure-garden, a shingle hut on the point of collapse which stands facing a pompous palace—how swiftly this brings down my soaring pride! My imagination completes the picture. I now see the curses of thousands teeming like a mass of voracious worms in this braggart world of decomposition. Everything that was elevated and charming becomes repellent to me. I realize that it is nothing more than a diseased, wasting body whose eyes and cheeks burn with the hectic hues of fever and feign a flourishing life, while gangrene and putrefaction rage in the expiring lungs. (v. 879)

The grandeur of that damning vision harks back to an earlier Baroque rhetoric and points forward to the political cartoons of a journalistic age just dawning, it combines the anger of a social critic with the fervour of a born preacher; but its organizing image is the work specifically of a medical mind trained to observe fever symptoms and diagnose the inner decline.

But who and what was Schiller to have and declare such a vision? That was a question he had been compelled to ask himself in the summer of 1784. His year's contract at Mannheim was running out and there were clear signs it would not be renewed. For Dalberg he was a dubious asset, potentially even a liability. For one thing he had not delivered the agreed third play within the year. For another, anything he did deliver needed changing, toning down. Meanwhile there were other writers who seemed not to have problems meeting deadlines: the rising theatrical star Iffland, who as an actor had created the role of Franz Moor, also had a talent for putting together plays which appealed to audiences but did not have the disturbing side-effect Schiller's had of stimulating critical reflection on life and society. Such inert bourgeois tragedies were much preferable for anyone who both thought in the short term and wanted a quiet life, both of which applied to Dalberg. There were political pressures to get rid of Schiller which came from outside the theatre, and there were intrigues against him from within. A comedy played in Mannheim that year actually contained a caricature of a wild and indecisive poet, Patchword; everyone knew who that was. The sensational success of *The Robbers* was far in the past. Schiller was once again in a precarious position and without prospects. It was the moment to rise to an act of self-reaffirmation.

He did so in June 1784 in an address to a Mannheim cultural society entitled 'The Effect of Theatre on the People' (*Vom Wirken der Schaubühne auf das Volk*; later given the less dynamic, sententious-sounding title 'The Theatre considered as a Moral Institution'). Many of Schiller's points are familiar currency of the day, claims made for theatre either before or in response to Rousseau's radical attack on it in the famous *Letter to Monsieur d'Alembert* (1758)—for example, that theatre has a sharper impact than philosophical argument or preaching, that it extends morality beyond the clear-cut questions on which religion and law pre- or proscribe, and that it offers a 'school of practical wisdom'. Then there are some specifically German concerns, also much talked about, namely that dramatists should choose German subjects, should help create a national theatre in the fullest sense, in the hope that a common culture might somehow turn this fragmented people into a nation. (Mannheim, like Hamburg and Vienna before it, prematurely claimed the title 'National' for the theatre it had just—in 1779—established.)

But Schiller's opening paragraphs contain the more personal question posed by his self-respect: 'whether the business to which we are devoting the best part of our mental powers is compatible with the dignity of our spirit'. In other words, has he been following his true vocation? For only 'when we have decided in our own minds what we are and what we are not, only then have we escaped the danger of suffering from other's opinions, of being bloated by their praise or rendered cowardly by their disparagement' (v. 818)—just the extremes Schiller had now experienced in unpleasant sequence. And if that was a meditation addressed to himself, there is open defiance when he speaks of the 'small minds that take revenge on genius' and

33

'condemn the young man who, driven by an inner force, steps out of the narrow prison of his livelihood and follows the voice of the god within him' (v. 819).

Asserting independence in adversity later became the nub of Schiller's tragic theory. It is plainly rooted in his experience and practice of living. He does of course have authorities he can draw on to sustain his faith. When he says that 'theatre is the communal channel into which the light of wisdom streams down from the thinking better section of the people and thence is diffused in milder beams through the whole state', or that 'the mist of barbarism, of grim superstition vanishes, darkness yields to victorious light' (v. 828), this is the standard Enlightenment doctrine of benevolent aristocratic intellect serving society, and it is dressed in standard rhetorical form.

Yet where Schiller treats the human mechanisms that come into play at the theatrical point of delivery, and when he talks about the sensation which the spectator (or, better, the participant) feels, the ideas are more characteristically his own, reminiscent again of his medical thinking and shaped by an impulse that is not so much aristocratic as democratic and communitarian; while the rhetoric that conveys them takes on a note of almost Romantic enthusiasm.

Theatre he presents as part of the answer to a fundamental need felt by human beings who are torn between, and in different ways worn out by, the demands of physical and mental existence:

> Our nature, equally incapable of continuing longer in the animal [i.e. physical] state or of persisting with the subtler work of the understanding, demanded a midway condition which would unite both these contradictory extremes, tone down their harsh tension to a gentle harmony and make possible the transition from either state to the other. This function is fulfilled by the aesthetic sense, or the feeling for beauty. (v. 821)

The argument looks back to the 'medial force' of the *Philosophy of Physiology*, but it also already has the shape—clear and simple, though susceptible of immense refinement in detail—of Schiller's mature aesthetics. The peroration then enlarges this central conception and turns analysis into vision in one of the great passages of German eighteenth-century prose which, for all its period flavour, retains its power to move us if we still have any faith in art:

> The theatre is the place where pleasure joins with instruction, relaxation with concentration, amusement with education, where no capacity of the mind is extended to the detriment of the others, no pleasure enjoyed at the cost of the totality. When worry eats at our hearts, when gloomy moods poison our solitude, when the world and its affairs revolt us, when a thousand burdens press on our spirit and our responses threaten to suffocate under our professional labours, theatre is there to receive us—in this artificial world we can dream the real world away, we are restored to ourselves, our sensibilities awaken, salutary passions stir our somnolent nature and drive the blood in more vigorous pulses. If people are unhappy, here they can weep out their sorrow in compassion with the sorrow of others; those who are blithely happy are sobered, the complacent made to think again. The soft and sentimental acquire a manly hardness, the crude and unfeeling become sensitive for the first time. And then finally, what a triumph for nature—nature so often downtrodden, so often arising again—when men and women of all circles and zones and classes, every fetter of falsity and fashion thrown off, torn free from the pressures of fate, joined in brotherhood by one all-embracing sympathy, dissolved back into one family, oblivious of themselves and the world, again come near to their heavenly origin. Each of them enjoys the delights of all, which a hundred eyes render back stronger and finer, and each individual breast has room for only one emotion—that of being human. (v. 831)

Many other eighteenth-century writers believed theoretically in our common humanity, and thought art a useful medium for showing it—at a distance on the stage. None of them envisaged scenes which would put that belief into practice in the auditorium, certainly not with such a radical and almost dionysian abandonment of everything that overlays our common humanity and protects us from other people's. But then, none of them had experienced—much less been responsible for—a theatrical sensation like the first night of *The Robbers*.

2 Hope in history

Castles in Spain

Two months after that apotheosis of theatre, Schiller lost his own. He had tried desperately to sell himself to Mannheim again, promising Dalberg great and new things: anyone could write bourgeois tragedy but not everyone could rise to historical drama in the grand manner, which he now said was his true calling—and incidentally a type of work that would bring a theatre greater prestige than the more banal bourgeois genre. Nor would his historical subject, he reassured Dalberg, be at all political, but rather a 'family portrait in a royal house' (letters of 7 June and 24 Aug. 1784). This was to treat in Dalberg's preferred way a subject he himself had put Schiller on to, in a romanticized version of Spanish history by the Abbé St Réal: Carlos, Prince of Spain, tragically loves the woman originally meant for him but then married by his father Philip II—loves, that is, his 'mother' and is rejected by his father, whose jealousy leads to the son's death.

Schiller's proffered novelties and diplomatic compliance got him nowhere; his contract was not renewed. Dalberg had also turned down his earlier offer to write a monthly house-journal of play-reviews and general essays on drama and its development in Mannheim, an emulation of Lessing's great critical series of the 1760s, *Drama in Hamburg* (*Hamburgische Dramaturgie*). Schiller was forced to contemplate going back to medicine, which would earn him more than his pen seemed likely to if once he qualified fully. Or might he even (an impossibly sanguine scheme for combining both careers) induce Dalberg to pay for his final year of medical study in return for a promise of more plays later . . . ? But there had been difficulty enough getting completed plays out of a full-time house-poet. Schiller was left again without visible means of support. Still, he had some editorial experience from Württemberg days, so he expanded his 'Drama in Mannheim' plan into a general journal of literary and local interest and launched it single-handed as author, editor, and publisher. He hoped to attract five hundred firm subscribers.

The market was not favourable. In eighteenth-century Germany young hopefuls were always starting short-lived journals. Schiller's publicity leaflet 'Announcing the *Rhineland Thalia*' (v. 854 ff.) faces the fact that the country is awash with journals that have not lived up to public expectations. But he appeals to the public nevertheless to give him its 'blind trust'—not so much for what he plans to publish as for what and who he is, and for the relation in which he stands to the public. For he writes 'as a citizen of the world who serves no prince', as one whose literary strivings conflicted from the start with an oppressive system, and whose first play 'cost [him] family and fatherland'. With those connections severed, 'the public is everything to me, my study, my sovereign, my confidant . . . A grand feeling comes over me at the thought that I wear no other fetter than the verdict of the world, that I appeal to no other throne than the human mind.' It is a classic Enlightenment statement, and not just by virtue of the grand cosmopolitanism which a small move from Stuttgart to Mannheim had allowed. Enlightenment writers had spread the notion that 'the public' meant not merely the commercial market but a free market of ideas. The members of society were thought of as an audience that would keenly follow, and if need be join in, a continuing debate on problems of their common life, especially how to improve the way things were done in society. No one had better credentials to be heard in that forum than Schiller the fugitive from absolutism, just as no one had a more obvious psychological need to embrace its liberal authority than Schiller the rootless exile. But if he was to survive, he had to solve the problem that faced the whole class of would-be independent writers then just emerging, namely how to make that audience put its money where its social and intellectual concerns were—in other words, how to make the 'market' support the 'forum'. In best Enlightenment fashion, Schiller was opening his pages to 'every subject that interests Mankind in general and relates to its happiness'; his Enlightenment devotion to 'the public' was passionate (perhaps also calculatedly flattering). But he was also, as in *The Effect of Theatre on the People*, again going beyond Enlightenment positions and demanding from his audience a deeper, even an intimate involvement. For he ends by saying that he will only value subscriptions to the *Rhineland Thalia* if they spring from a 'personal sympathy' for the writer behind the works, for the writer as *more valuable* than the works. His overriding aim is 'to forge between myself and the public a bond of friendship'. Success is to be secured not just by Enlightenment credentials but by Romantic charisma.

A more down-to-earth speculation on the literary market somewhat later was a novel for serialization in the *Thalia* (1787–9). *The Visionary* is a melodramatic mystery-story about Catholic machinations aimed at the conversion of a Protestant prince. But Schiller's heart was not in the project for long, and he finally abandoned it unfinished. The trouble was that the public devoured the novel for its sensational subject-matter and Schiller was discontented with mere pot-boiler success—even though financially that was just what he needed and had been aiming at. In one way he was right to be fastidious about the story's reception: it deserves reading for less crude reasons, as a brilliant exercise in the narrative structuring and variation of stylistic pace that generate suspense.

Meantime the higher speculation on the 'friendship' of the public seemed to have failed. Schiller's impassioned appeal had won the journal precious few subscribers. Yet he was then rescued through very much the sort of personal sympathy he had hoped for, if by a different route. A letter from four young admirers—Christian Gottfried Körner, Ludwig Ferdinand Huber, and their fiancées Minna and Dora Stock—led to correspondence, correspondence to a prompt invitation, and in the spring of 1785 Schiller joined them. For the next eighteen months, he was their guest in Leipzig and Dresden, and Körner effectively his patron. For example, when Schiller, sanguine as ever, reckoned on an annual eight or nine hundred taler clear profit from his journal but needed a Leipzig publisher to take it on and also advance him three hundred to settle his Mannheim debts, it was Körner who secretly secured the publisher Göschen (one of whose substantial shareholders he was) and advanced the sum himself. Körner's help was not always secret, but was always discreet: 'I know that by working just for your livelihood you can meet all your needs. But for one year at least allow me the pleasure of freeing you from that necessity' (8 July 1785). That first sentence was barely even true—Schiller's first three plays were briskly reprinting, but the publishers were paying him not a penny: there was no copyright law to observe. He accepted Körner's support without fuss. The heady tones of friendship in their early letters may now seem quaint, but nothing lessens the value of Körner's generosity. It was an extraordinary personal initiative in the difficult historical interim between court patronage and the establishment of a properly regulated literary market. Like the legacy from Raisley Calvert which set Wordsworth free to be a poet, this was bourgeois help for a bourgeois writer, disinterested in a way noble patronage rarely was.

Friendship was meanwhile becoming one of the major themes of Schiller's new play. His Spanish subject had been inherently unstable from the start: how could the author of *The Robbers* and *Intrigue and Love* treat Philip II's domestic life and not get drawn into the larger political questions of sixteenth-century Spain? Before ever Schiller told Dalberg that there would be no politics this time, he was in fact planning to include in his 'family portrait' such undomestic figures as 'a cruel, hypocritical Inquisitor and a barbaric Duke of Alva' and to avenge humanity at large by pillorying the Inquisition (to Reinwald, 27 March and 14 April 1783). It was hardly even a matter of choosing to include this or that distinct figure or topic; the love-and-jealousy plot had an inherent structure and direction of growth, an organic potential. It set youth against age, nature against convention and ceremonial, human feeling against dynastic politics, innocence against surveillance, trust against suspicion, freedom against constraint—all fundamental social issues for an eighteenth-century (or any) idealist, and familiar ground already from Schiller's previous plays. But of those plays only one (*Fiesco*) had a historical subject, and that a relatively obscure episode which was part of no greater movement. This time the structuring antitheses of the drama had as their background the first great rebellion of modern Europe and the first defeat of absolutism. History on the grandest scale reached into the claustrophobic court setting, not as an alien thing but as a larger embodiment of the personal issues—or so it could be seen and shown. Showing it so, linking the general and the particular, was ultimately the problem Schiller wrestled with for the four and a half years of a changing conception. That makes the genesis of *Don Carlos* (1787) almost as intricate and absorbing as the action itself.

From being the centre of attention for its own sake, Carlos's love for Elisabeth becomes a means to an end; it is sublimated into the motive force for his political commitment to free the Dutch provinces. From being a brooding Hamlet-figure, Carlos becomes an idealistic activist. That strand is further strengthened and the emphasis of the whole play shifts away from Carlos when Schiller takes a minor figure from Louis Sebastien Mercier's *Portrait de Philippe II d'Espagne* of 1785, and makes him the play's intellectual centre. As Carlos's friend and confidant, Marquis Posa nurtures the principles of the future king, who is the best hope for a changed Spain. He also, riskily if not inconsistently, pursues a plan to get Carlos to the Netherlands as leader of the rebellion; and he protects the Queen against intrigue and suspicion, because she is to be the energy behind Carlos's commitment. Even the jealousy motif opens into politics. Symbolically the estrangement of father and son mirrors that of the royal 'father' and his subjects; and in plot terms, the King's doubt whether any courtier will tell him the truth about the Queen makes him turn to the man of integrity, Posa. That gives Idealism direct access to the ear of Power and Schiller the chance, as we shall see, for a grand dramatic confrontation. What the play does not grow to embrace is political action itself. Goethe's *Egmont*, a play on the same phase of history, and published by a curious coincidence the year after *Don Carlos*, takes us to the open streets and squares as well as castles of the Netherlands. Schiller's play remains a closet-drama about the ideas and motives that determine a distant actuality. Nevertheless, our knowledge of the practical outcome—Philip's long failure and the dogged resistance of the Dutch—is vital. The Rise of the Dutch Republic is one of history's moral success-stories, which means that Schiller's tragic ending, with Posa killed and Carlos handed over to the Inquisition, is set in a framework of hope. That in turn means that the play's high idealism, with its grand rhetorical expression, rings a good deal less hollow than it otherwise might have done. It has a basis in reality from which to answer political 'realists' and their self-fulfilling assumptions about the limits human nature sets to political ideals.

There are other reasons why *Don Carlos* rings essentially true (disregarding, that is, the invention of a Carlos quite unlike his grotesque original). Schiller matured with his play. His 1783 intention to pillory Alva and the Inquisition promised a moral diatribe, and for Enlightenment writers Philip himself was the classic villain: arch-absolutist, champion of a blood-thirsty Counter-Reformation, *aficionado* of the *auto-da-fé* who reputedly said he would build the pyre himself if his own son became a heretic. Dramatic treatment only needed to orchestrate such formulas of self-condemnation for an eighteenth-century audience to be appropriately shocked. That is what Mercier did in his play. It was the kind of thing Schiller had done in *Intrigue and Love*: 'When I enter, a principality trembles,' says the President (i. 776), and Wurm declares his own moral nullity by scorning the bourgeois for their high principles, which his plan depends on. Yet by 1785, when Schiller published the original Act I of *Don Carlos* in the *Rhineland Thalia*, he was already outgrowing the partisan simplicities of satire. His foreword to this first instalment of a still largely unwritten play marks the first kink in the genesis, with an admission that he has lost his inspiration and would appreciate readers' comments. More importantly, he recognizes that to shock an audience with the horrors of Carlos and Elisabeth's situation was simple—but was shock (*Erschütterung*) the emotion he wanted to produce? And then, astoundingly:

> If this tragedy is to move people [*rühren*] it must do so, it seems to me, through the situation and character of King Philip. Perhaps the whole weight of the tragedy rests on the way that is treated . . . People expect I know not what monster when they hear the name Philip—my play collapses the moment they find a figure like that in it, and yet I hope to remain true to history. (ii. 222 f.)

A moving King Philip and fidelity to history? The seeming contradiction marks a great step forward for Schiller's art. The satirical moralist pointing the finger at his own puppets becomes the historical dramatist who is prepared to enter into the humanity of those humanity abhors. That is by no means to say that he has sold out to neutrality and will cherish the ruthless *Realpolitiker* as he does the rebellious idealists, much less condone his ruthlessness. But he will make ruthlessness plausible from within, see the world through its eyes, and take what he sees seriously. His characters' (and his own) counter-view will be the more finely tempered for having to argue at full intellectual stretch with evil, instead of enjoying a moral walkover. An evil system will be more convincingly evil as a system if its agents are shown to act in grim good faith. This is how Schiller portrays them. It is because their Catholic belief is absolute that they reduce the people they rule over to ciphers of no independent value, and meet the Dutch situation with ruthless measures, not humane magnanimity. The strong hand (Alva pointedly reminds Carlos) is what won and held the lands and crown Carlos will inherit:

> This sword
> Wrote Spanish laws for foreign peoples, went
> Glittering ahead and cleared the way for Christ,
> Carved out the bloody furrows for the seed
> Of faith to grow in on this continent.
> God judged in Heaven, and I judged on earth.   (1422 ff.)

That is not self-condemnation contrived by an outraged satirist, but the language of conviction imagined by a true dramatist. Schiller's empathy finds a chillingly authentic voice for the defenders of the *status quo*, in a rising scale from Alva via Philip to the Inquisitor. He, aged and blind, dominates the stage at the close. The King shrinks into powerlessness and even the free spirit Posa turns out to have been all along under the hand of the Inquisition. Only death has saved him from the torture and forced recantation with which the Inquisitor planned publicly to defile 'boastful reason' (lines 5179 ff.). This authority higher than royal power now demands from Philip the sacrifice of Carlos, an unloved son but still a son:

KING: It would be
  Sinning against nature—can your power silence
  Even that mighty voice?
INQUISITOR: Faith does not hear
  The voice of nature [. . .] Give him
  To me.
KING: He is my only son—what, who
  Have I worked and built for?
INQUISITOR: For decomposition
  Sooner than freedom.

                                          (5271 ff.)

That may be, in the terms of Schiller's first conception ('a cruel, hypocritical Inquisitor'), 'cruel' to the point of fanaticism, but it is not 'hypocritical'.

In defeat Carlos and Posa become martyrs for a faith which does hear the 'mighty voice of nature'. Its message is conveyed through contrast with the human corruption and distortion shown throughout the play, but it is also expressed directly. If the dramatist's empathy gives a hearing to the bleak vision of politic men, his own passionate commitment demands a chance for Posa to state the philosophy of freedom and implore Philip to transform the political world starting with his own empire. As Schiller's most celebrated set piece, the 'audience scene' has suffered from parody, post-liberal fatigue, and the kind of familiarity that forgets how good a classic piece of writing actually is—forgets also how deftly the Grand Statement is grafted on the action. Posa's opportunity grows out of the plot and itself crystallizes the issues that underlie the debate with Philip: the King's isolation and suffering make him need a human being he can trust—but humanity and trust have been destroyed by the system he maintains and the court he is enclosed by. He can only turn to the rare exception who has stayed uncorrupted, which gives an opening to an alternative vision of life and implicitly begins to recognize its value.

Posa has already distinguished himself in the King's service, but withdrawn without seeking any high office as reward. Philip, for whom self-seeking among his subjects is axiomatic, probes for the reasons. Posa, unprepared and feeling his way (can he put his thoughts as a 'citizen of this world' into words a subject may speak to a king?) is half-pressed, half-coaxed into the admission: 'I cannot be the servant of a prince' (line 3020). He fills the shocked silence with his reasons, which effectively reject monarchy as a form of government: it uses human beings as mere instruments and measures the value of what they do wholly by royal praise and reward, whereas Posa would wish his actions to have intrinsic value. In the background is Montesquieu's distinction that the principle of monarchies is honour, of republics virtue; and Posa's enthusiasm adds warmth to the cool concept 'virtue' when he says 'I love/ Humanity, and monarchies will let/ Me only love myself' (3035 ff.).

Posa has so far questioned social form, not substance, leaving the King's image of himself and his purposes unshaken. But he now refuses the offer of any post in Philip's realms from which to 'do good'. For what kind of good could that be? In Spain the only 'human happiness' permitted is what the crown can afford, just as the only truth allowed is what the crown itself has coined for circulation. In contrast, the happiness Posa conceives for people 'would make a monarch tremble' (3044 ff.). The metaphor of coinage is telling: Philip has set a uniform stamp on a precious metal; the progressive argues, paradoxically, for a return to its pristine state. Philip, prompt and simplistic as a McCarthy committee sniffing out Communist subversives, exclaims 'You are a Protestant.' When Posa assures him he is a Catholic and loyal, the King switches to cynicism: this boldness must be a novel courtier's tactic tried on in place of worn-out flattery. That at least recognizes what the usual effects of Philip's regime are, and lets Posa press home the point that a system which deifies one man makes willing slaves of the rest (3090 ff.).

But it does even worse to the unwilling:

I have just come from Flanders and Brabant.
So many blossoming, rich provinces!
A sturdy people, a great and a good
People—and to be father of that people!
That, I thought, that must be divine! And then
I came upon piles of burnt human bones.   (3135 ff.)

Posa, like Schiller, tries even in the face of atrocity to understand tyranny from within, its perception of necessity, its ability to carry out the terrible acts this perception entails. That
a mere human being can do what 'must' be done forces a shud-
dering admiration from Posa, even while he speaks of gentler
centuries to come when 'States will no longer squander their
own children, / And their necessity will be humane' (3152 f.).

Political divergence here becomes, as it ultimately must, a
conflict between theories of history. For Philip, those gentler
centuries can only come if he combats the 'curse' of the present:
implacable violence is the only path to peace. For Posa, the only
peace repression can achieve is the peace of the graveyard: Philip
is trying to raise a future from seeds of death. Meantime real
growth, change and movement are everywhere, a 'universal
springtime' is renewing Christendom (is Posa *really* not a Protestant?), the world is being reshaped, the wheel is rolling too fast
for human hand to seize it by the spokes. At the same time—
something more concrete than these metaphors—Spain is
depleting itself and enriching its rivals as persecution drives
productive citizens into exile; so tyranny even defeats its own
objects. History is against Philip, he is fighting nature itself as
he destroys and compels in a world that is designed to work on
the principle of freedom. The 'freedom of thought' which Posa's
most famous line begs Philip to grant, is a necessary part of
nature's system, whose divine master does not intervene to
constrain or prohibit. Nature 'is founded / On freedom—and
how rich it is through freedom' (3216 f.). Yet even now Philip
need not go down in history as a Nero ('that pains me; for / You
were good', 3190 f.). He can join the true movement of history
and create a new earth at the stroke of a pen if he will only
reverse his violation of nature: 'Give back / What you have
taken from us', 'Restore mankind's / Long-lost nobility. Let

citizens / Again be what they were before, the crown's / Prime purpose' (3240 ff.). The 'new earth' would in fact be an old, a restored earth. This is the politics of paradise lost, Elysium, the state of nature, a new and purified social contract; it is ideal-istic, unpolitical in any normal sense of the word, *Idealpolitik* in place of *Realpolitik*. For Philip, and for anyone who is convinced by his dismissive words—'You will think otherwise when once you know / Men as I know them' (3291 f.)—it is an impossible vision. But that does not make it a mere emotional outburst by a still immature poet, overdone and out of date. On the contrary, human beings persist in hoping that politics may yet become precisely the art of the impossible. The potential of nature goes on being the real base for a dreamt-of fresh start in human affairs. Writing that can touch so permanent a chord in our sensibilities, and so permanent a discord in our relation to the world, is still very much alive. Nor is the high generality of Posa's speeches an objection. Drama is not the medium for spelling out detailed proposals for reform. It can legitimately keep to the clashing principles that shape (or twist) society and its institutions.

Of course in one sense the audience scene is an impossible dialogue. The historical Philip would not have heard Posa out, and no sixteenth-century Posa could have stated the principles of eighteenth-century liberal thought. These were a later prod-uct of the forces only just beginning to stir in the Dutch struggle for liberty. The scene is an anachronism, a virtuoso piece of *esprit de l'escalier* across a gulf of time. But to say this would be trivial if it did not lead on to the positive point that historical drama is not merely, sometimes not even primarily, a recon-struction of the past so much as a means to understand and speak to the present. Posa's audience with Philip is really aimed at the other, contemporary audience of which Schiller had such a clear and ambitious conception. In that forum it is in a sense Philip who becomes the anachronism, an acute reminder of the scores of anachronisms who were still, two centuries after him, ruling over German States large and small, untrammelled by constitution or conscience, in principle left behind by the pro-gress of enlightened thought yet in practice left in place by the more sluggish course of history. The Rise of a German Republic was nowhere in sight.

Not that Posa's message, for all its republican sympathies, is quite as revolutionary as it seems. He looks forward to a reconciliation of King and Subject—a constitutional monarchy, that is. His plan for Carlos to lead the Dutch, albeit in rebellion, is meant to maintain the legitimist principle but add to it the intrinsic legitimacy of a new political vision. In fostering this and in arguing with Philip's intransigence, Posa stands less in the line of modern revolutionaries than in an older tradition of would-be educators and philosophic advisers to the powerful. From Plato's adventure with Dionysius of Syracuse and Aristotle's tutorship of Alexander the Great, down to Erasmus's *Education of a Christian Prince* written in 1516 for Carlos's grandfather the Emperor Charles V, the idea was kept alive that better government would come about if future rulers could be caught and taught early enough, or if present rulers could be induced to open their minds to philosophy. In Schiller's own day much Enlightenment ingenuity went into persuading the powerful that it was in their interest, in a practical or some higher sense, to temper *raison d'état* with reason pure and simple.

Posa gets the chance to be both educator and adviser. Maybe, as Schiller said (ii. 253), a play cannot show a whole education (German writers were later to adapt the novel to that purpose). But Posa revives ideals which have their roots in Carlos's education and thereby continues the education unhappy love has diverted him from. As a student at Alcalá, Carlos dreamt of being the 'creator of another Golden Age / In Spain' (176 f.). But when Posa has failed with the King and death threatens, he reverts to his first project and leaves his political testament for the Queen to pass on to Carlos: the Prince must set his hand to the 'unhewn stone' of political change, however hopeless the task seems for one lifetime, and keep faith with his youthful dreams even when the 'deadly insect of so-called sounder reason' attacks that divine flower (4279 ff.).

But precisely Posa's tactical switches tangle and betray his personal loyalties and confidences, in a fourth Act which is itself so tangled that few readers feel they quite grasp its twists and turns. From being a friend and confidant, Posa becomes a manipulator of both father and son (the Queen he has been manipulating all along). Using people, who should be ends in themselves, as Schiller understood before ever he read Kant's ethics, was what Posa objected to in Philip. Posa has himself been corrupted by political opportunism. He ceases to be a shining hero and becomes as problematic as his opposite, the King. Schiller had extended his imaginative range to make a tyrant seem human; he extends it further to show the flaws in an idealist. That such people may be so devoted to the cause of humanity that they treat human beings inhumanely is an insight that reaches beyond the play. It is part of a typological theory Schiller was to develop later, and it was soon to be an element in French revolutionary practice: as with the ethics of violent rebellion in *The Robbers*, there was something prophetic in Schiller's portrayal of the ethics of political idealism.

Artistically, *Don Carlos* is both a triumph and a failure, a breakthrough and a warning. On the positive side, Schiller had created as if from nowhere a dramatic medium of great emotional power and flexibility. His prose dialogue in earlier plays had worked by overstatement, using a rhetoric of caricatures and climaxes. Now, paradoxically, he achieves naturalness through verse and gets effects through restraint; the unrhymed iambic pentameters absorb vehemence and smooth away melodramatic gesture. That goes hand in hand with the less black-and-white characterization; indeed it may have been the new medium as much as any purely intellectual maturing that made it impossible to portray Philip as a 'monster', so closely is the conception of a character bound up with the tone in which he is to speak. This new balance (which incidentally settles the conflict between 'English' freedom and French classical control in the literary scene and soul of eighteenth-century Germany) was to be Schiller's form for life.

In contrast, the structure of *Don Carlos* runs to unmanageable excess. If the verse has moved towards the classical, the handling of plot is deeply Romantic. Dramatic functionality takes second place to fullness of expression. The *Thalia* fragment of 1785, only three acts, is already 4,040 lines or some 125 pages long. The full first edition of 1787 is over six thousand. Even the canonical final text, revised in 1801, still has more than five thousand lines, or some 210 pages—well over twice the length of a normal play. Sub-plots expand into digressions; it takes a dozen pages to create and clear up a misunderstanding between Carlos and Princess Eboli (Act II. Sc. 1) which will later be lengthily renarrated to Posa, for over-intricate action demands passages of explanation to help the characters (let alone the spectators) understand it. Above all, as the focus shifts from Carlos and Elisabeth to Carlos and Posa and then to Posa and Philip, from love to politics and then to the bizarre emotional politics of the last act, space is needed to work out each new set of psychological complexities. The size problem, in other words, is only the outward symptom of changing conceptions which left no firm ground for a unified and concise structure to stand on. 'The work necessarily shared in the vicissitudes my way of thinking and feeling underwent in this period', Schiller wrote (ii. 226). Time had undone art.

Worse, it might do so again as long as Schiller's approach to art did not alter. His grand theory of creativity, human and divine, was one of love arising from loneliness and impelling both God and the artist to project themselves into creatures that would reflect them. 'Every poetic work is essentially an enthusiastic friendship or platonic love for a creation of our own mind . . . All products of our imagination are ultimately *ourselves*. The poet must be not so much the portraitist of his hero—he must be rather his *beloved*, his *bosom-friend*' (to Reinwald, 14 April 1783). Intimacy then, to the point of identification—why else does Karl Moor, otherwise a paragon of heroic good looks, turn out to have a 'goose neck' (i. 572), and why else did Schiller want him played only by a tall, gaunt actor (i. 637), if not to match his own famously gawky appearance? Similarly, it was clear to Abel as he heard Schiller declaim from his second play that the playwright dreamt of being Fiesco. His early heroes have to be young (even Fiesco, the *dramatis personae* stipulates, is only twenty-three) and Schiller admits that he grew out of his sympathy for Carlos as he outgrew him in age (ii. 226). Any delay in composition risked breaking vital links. A new identification meant seeing the dramatic situation from a different angle, reshaping an established plot to carry a new theme. Schiller's method could only work when a play was, figuratively if not literally, 'the blossom of a single summer' (ii. 227), i.e. a unified organic growth. And even then, it was at odds with the accepted nature of drama as an objective genre which demands a quite different, paradoxically a detached involvement with all the characters at once and within the bounds of settled plot-relations. A play's 'message' then normally arises from the whole nexus of a completed action. True, Schiller's characterization in *Don Carlos* had moved beyond simple identification, but too late to rescue the play's cohesion. Its disunity was the *reductio ad absurdum* of Schiller's early way of writing. He tried to save the situation by writing a series of *Letters on Don Carlos*, explaining how the themes had grown out of one another. But genetic explanation was a doubtful substitute for formal achievement, not to say an admission of defeat.

Schiller had meantime made career capital from the unfinished play. He gave a reading of Act I before Karl August, Duke of Weimar, asked for and received the minor honorary title of *Hofrat* (Court Councillor), and dedicated the *Thalia* fragment to this 'noblest of Germany's princes' (ii. 220). That scarcely squares with the claim he had just made when launching the journal that, like Posa, he was not the servant of any prince. But there were realities as well as idealities. He had to survive. His reputation as a rebel was probably a wasting asset—look how few *Thalia* subscribers it had brought in. He could not live for ever on Körner's charity. Cultural influence was still largely in princely hands. This particular prince was at least 'the sensitive friend of the Muses' (ii. 220) and patron of Johann Wolfgang Goethe. The favour of Karl August would publicly offset the earlier bother with Karl Eugen. A writer needed solid ground under his feet. Perhaps the Duchy of Weimar was where it might be found.

A guiding thread

Weimar was indeed Schiller's final destination, but the way there was not through literature proper. *Don Carlos* had drawn him into history. In autumn 1785 he translated the long historical introduction to Mercier's play. By spring 1786 history was growing 'daily more precious' to him (to Körner, 15 April). By August he was planning to edit a series of volumes on *The History of the most Remarkable Rebellions and Conspiracies*, a commercial speculation in the main, but having clear affinities with his work so far (and with much that was still to come). Naturally he kept the Dutch Revolt to do himself. It soon began to grow under his hands (to Crusius, 6 March 1787) and with it his ambition to make his mark as a historian (to Körner, 18 Aug. 1787). Study gave him pleasure, but part of the pleasure was the sense that he was producing 'something *solid*' in contrast to the 'libertinism of literature', as an unenlightened actual public would judge it (to Körner, 19 Dec. 1787). 'Solid' work led to something more solid yet. Volume one of *The Revolt of the United Netherlands against Spanish Rule* (all that ever appeared of a projected six) came out in autumn 1786 and by December Schiller had the offer of a chair in history at Jena from the Weimar authorities. That was still not very solid—it carried no salary, only the right to charge for private teaching—but it was meant from the outset to lead to higher things. Till it did, the Professor of History would have to live by writing history, at a rate (Schiller calculated) of just six taler for a week's hard reading and writing (to Huber, 25 Dec. 87).

Early in their friendship Körner wrote that 'all the greatness of character and situation that history offers and Shakespeare has not exhausted, waits for your brush. It is so to speak a commission' (11 Jan. 1785). But he meant drama, not this kind of drudgery. He thought his friend was prostituting his talent on what Schiller admitted were 'works of diligence', not 'works of genius' (to Körner 1 Dec. 1788). In an immediate sense perhaps he was, but ultimately historical study was spadework for that greater commission as an artist. Schiller was intensely aware of his own ignorance about the world, he felt the deficiencies of his education acutely. Reading history was one way of absorbing outside reality. More specifically, it offered him a 'storehouse to draw on' (to Körner, 27 July 1788). Something else too gave the hard historical grind an element of spiritual commitment: while writing the *Revolt*, Schiller read Kant.

His debt to Kant is a commonplace of intellectual history, but almost all the critical attention has gone on aesthetics and tragic ethics. What Schiller first derived from Kant though—and what inspired him to study Kant intensively later—was a vision of history and a programme of historical research and exposition. In 1787 he read some short essays Kant had published in the celebrated *Berlin Monthly*, and was especially 'satisfied' by the one called *Idea for a General History with a Cosmopolitan Purpose* of 1784 (to Körner, 29 Aug. 1787). That bizarrely elaborate title prefaces a compact and luminous argument which starts from the way human behaviour shows statistical patterns beyond our individual intentions, and asks whether history too shows any such pattern. Taken singly, men's historical actions seem vain and destructive, making up a 'planless aggregate' ruled by 'blind chance'; mankind has outgrown instinct, but does not yet pursue an overall rational purpose. As a last resort for the philosophical observer, might the totality of human actions show some pattern of intention on the part of *nature*? If one could only make out a basic trend, some later writer might give a full account of nature's plan as manifested in the successive phases of history, much as Kepler's discoveries were later worked out into a full system by Newton. The historical observer making out the hopeful signs would be like the astronomer for whom even the slightest curve in a planet's trajectory is a clue to the regularity of an immense system.

The 'plan of nature' which Kant postulates is that the human race shall one day realize its full potential. It can only do this by trial and error through time, so only later generations will benefit fully. The means to nature's end are the contradictory human impulses on the one hand to form societies but on the other to be antagonistic—competitive, acquisitive, ambitious—within them. The evils this can lead to mean that mankind's biggest problem is how to achieve a just society which will control but not destroy those unlovable yet vital qualities and allow all human beings their full and free development. This problem *within* societies is then replicated *between* societies, i.e. states. Here the solution must one day be a league of nations (Kant actually invents that term). If nations do not choose this course rationally, they will come to it in the end through exhaustion and attrition by war. No sensible person can be content to take that long route once he has recognized nature's plan; he must surely try to further the plan with his own efforts. Thus a history of the world which convincingly showed the plan at work would speed up its accomplishment. Readers who believed in it, even provisionally, would contribute to new hopeful developments, which would strengthen their and others' faith, which in turn . . . An anything but vicious circle would result. History would help to make history. When Marx said that all the philosophers before him had aimed only to understand the world, not to change it, he was forgetting Kant.

Kant was whistling in the dark, and of course he knew it. He was not the first. For 'nature' read 'God', for 'the just society' read 'the City of God', and we are back with Christian theodicy, which had to justify the ways of God to man, an especially difficult task at times when persecution and other disasters blocked the larger perspective. This could only stand out clearly in the grand sweep of what Bossuet in 1681 was the first to call 'universal history'.

The difference between Bossuet and Kant is not just the replacement of an inscrutable God by an equally inscrutable nature. Bossuet's universal history is dogmatic, asserting the divine plan in history as a reality to be believed in literally: 'It is thus that God reigns over nations. Let us speak no more of chance or fortune, except as a name with which we cover our ignorance. What seems chance to our uncertain counsels is a concerted design to a higher, to that eternal counsel which contains all causes and effects in one single order' (Pt. III, ch. 8). By contrast, the universal history Kant proposes would be pragmatic, it would give human beings responsibility for making the 'plan of nature' real. Only if they achieve the just society and human fulfilment will the idea of a plan have been 'true' all along. Meantime they must act as if it is. It hangs in the balance as a fragile hypothesis, wishful thinking about the future based on a chosen way of seeing the past. Kant signals this very clearly by a recurrent image from the myth of Theseus and Ariadne: the idea of nature's plan is a 'guiding thread [*Leitfaden*] of reason', an '*a priori* guiding thread'—guiding us, that is, first through the labyrinth of past events and then ever more purposefully through the labyrinth of history still-to-be-made.

This purposeful view typified Enlightenment hope and practicality, but it had a new rival. Kant's former pupil at Königsberg, Herder, was now arguing that to subject generations and phases to some distant purpose was wrong. Though mankind as a whole might be only the bud of a flower which God had destined to blossom fully in the afterlife, each stage of earthly history, each separate culture, fulfilled meantime its *own* purpose and was of equal, not subordinate significance. Beliefs in a higher pattern—in rational and social progress—might be no more than peculiarities of their place and time; it was a kind of intellectual imperialism to subordinate other places and times to them. Historians should enter into the periods and civilizations they studied and try to understand each in its own terms (a doctrine which would become the foundation of modern anthropology.)

Perhaps Schiller was drawn to this approach. The year before reading Kant he lays it down that his series on *Rebellions and Conspiracies* will pay 'less attention to their universal influence than to the interest of detail and characters' (iv. 1009); but three years later his introduction to a series of historical memoirs argues that, for all their immediacy and colour, they must be related to 'the larger whole which they serve to clarify'; there is little use in even the most absorbing historical narrative if it does not refer the particular to the general and teach us how to apply it fruitfully (iv. 840 f.). Pattern is back in control.

Kant's grand scheme had an obvious appeal, as theory and as a call to action. Schiller had chafed at the social *status quo*, his heroes had dashed themselves against it, and the central audience scene in his still unfinished *Don Carlos* conjured up the movement of history in images full of hope—a universal spring time, a rolling wheel, mankind waking from slumber. What is more, he was already writing a history of the Dutch cause triumphant, to balance the tragedy of Posa and Carlos who fall as martyrs for that cause.

The Dutch revolt was as if made to fit into Kant's 'plan of nature'; for given the disproportion between Dutch and Spanish power, the happy outcome seemed providential, even miraculous (iv. 34 f.). But closer analysis showed how much 'providence' was a matter of favourable chance and the seizing of chances by men's resolute action. For example, when Philip's

despotism had shown its hand and inchoate rebellion was stirring in the Netherlands, but still 'the last perfecting touch
was missing—the perceptive and enterprising spirit who would
seize this great political moment and transform the gift of
chance into the plan of wisdom' (iv. 36), that was the cue for
William the Silent to enter. Equally decisive was failure to act
resolutely, as when Philip was slow to appear in person in the
Low Countries to counter unrest; this gave 'the work of chance
time to ripen into a work of the understanding' (iv. 42). Overall
the Dutch were offered more chances than the Spaniards, but
they also took them. Their actions thus came to compose
'nature's plan', even though, in first resisting Spanish authority, they never intended the grand liberation that finally came
about; the 'unseen hand of fate' intervened. Having given them
full credit for taking their chances, the philosopher-historian
then shifts the emphasis back to the raw material which was not
of their making: 'Man works, smoothes and shapes the unhewn
stone which the times bring into his reach; his is the moment
and the point, but it is chance that rolls world history along.' We
are not far from Trotsky's idea that the historical law is realized
through the natural selection of accidents, the workings of
chance being the random mutations which acquire evolution-
ary value when human beings exploit them. And when a historical episode is closed, we still have a choice, Schiller says, 'to
marvel at the dramatic birth of chance, or to pay our tribute of
admiration to a higher understanding' (iv. 44 f.). Providence is
not finally ruled out, though it stays as inscrutable as ever.

For Schiller it is also important what kind of people were
involved besides the great names. The Dutch were peaceable
fishermen, farmers, merchants: unlikely heroes, as far removed
as possible from the 'colossal beings' of earlier history to which
moderns look back as an old man does to the vigorous games of
youth (iv. 33 f.). This sounds at first like Karl Moor decrying the
impotence of his age. But Schiller's answer is now no longer
over-compensation by an outsize individualist. The small and
unheroic citizen can be effective if he will band together with
others; the Dutch have shown 'what can be dared for the good
cause and what can be achieved by uniting'. Schiller wants their
example—this is the activist element, applying the pattern of

the past to the history of the future—to give his equally unheroic readers 'an exhilarating sense of their own powers' (iv. 33); for 'the strength with which the Dutch people acted has not vanished from among us, the happy outcome that crowned their daring is not denied to us too if the times return and like occasions call us to like deeds' (iv. 1020). The impulse to human solidarity, glimpsed in the 'Ode to Joy' and *The Effect of Theatre on the People*, here becomes unambiguously political.

Not surprisingly, Schiller's inaugural lecture at Jena was on 'Universal history: what does it mean and to what end do we study it?' He appeals for a high philosophic approach, and offers those who are prepared to follow him beyond bread-and-butter studies a view of history as a single immense system of cause and effect where we can trace the forces that have shaped our present. He celebrates the relative stability and happiness of his own age which so many factors have conspired to produce, and ends by exhorting his student audience to pay their debt to the past by acting creatively on the future. Schiller's picture of the eighteenth century may seem naïve, a product of bourgeois complacency. But then comes a sophisticated paragraph on how such teleological thinking arises: the mind, hungry for harmony, begins to see in cause and effect a deliberate intention; the evidence for and against benevolent direction in history is weighed, and the observer finally plumps for the alternative that most gratifies the understanding and the emotions. Anyone who has seen that far into the psychology of historical hope can surely only entertain it on an 'as-if' basis. Yet in his peroration Schiller returns to the idea that there is a necessary course of history, not just as a postulate which men of good will must help to realize, but as an objective reality to which all human actions contribute, regardless of their conscious motives (iv. 766). He thus seems to oscillate between 'progress' as a regulative idea and as a literal belief. Either way, making plain the grand design is the vital public function of a historian.

Accordingly Schiller sets out to be Kant's Newton. The Jena philosopher Reinhold told Kant that 'the universal history he will create is designed on the lines of your plan, which he grasped with a purity and ardour that made him doubly dear to me' (14 June 1789). In his lectures Schiller began with the earliest human society, traced its development using the 'guiding thread' of the Mosaic books (iv. 767 ff.), moved thence to the Greece of Lycurgus and Solon, and aimed to sweep down through time so as to reach its eighteenth-century culmination within a single academic year (to Körner, 28 Sept. 1789). Likewise with the memoirs he was editing. He set each in a universal-history framework so as to show ultimate good emerging paradoxically from unfavourable circumstances. 'How different is Man's sowing from what fate allows him to reap!' (iv. 853). That is hardly a new or profound thought; yet successfully showing it at work in a concrete historical episode is probably what made Schiller express such intense satisfaction as he wrote his framework-essay on the Crusades (to Caroline von Beulwitz, 3 Nov. 1789). Amid all the raging religion and violence of that age, he saw superstition itself begin to undo the harm it had done mankind, as the meeting of two alien cultures set Europeans on the long road to relativism and tolerance (iv. 844 f., 853). Similarly, the barbarian invasions of Europe refreshed and renewed an exhausted culture (iv. 847); the Christian heroism of the knights of Malta showed an idea dominating human emotions, exercising the sinews of a future rationality (iv. 992 f.); and in the Reformation, convictions stronger than mere personal or national interest made men actually fight for ideas that scholars had arrived at in the study (iv. 849). The 'spirit of order' shows through in even the most terrible of historical events (iv. 851), the 'slow plant' of Enlightenment grows (iv. 849). History is too grim for facile optimism, but purposive enough for hope.

Besides these virtuoso sketches with their astronomer's-eye-view and their agile leaps from one historical episode to another, Schiller was soon engaged on his most substantial historical project, an account of the Thirty Years War which Carlyle was to call the most impressive performance to date by any German historian. All this left him too burdened to think of a new drama. He was in any case still recovering from the trauma of *Don Carlos* and its drawn-out genesis. To avoid similar problems recurring, he began a systematic study of aesthetics—a strangely abstract means to a concrete artistic end, but he felt his problem was a loss of spontaneity through too much reflection, and prescribed himself a homeopathic cure: 'Criticism must now make good the damage it has done me,' he wrote a little later, 'and damaged me it certainly has . . . I now *see* myself creating, I observe the play of inspiration, and my imagination proceeds with less freedom now it knows it has witnesses. But if I can once reach the point where *artifice* again becomes *nature* . . . then the imagination will get its old freedom back' (to Körner, 25 May 1792). Once more, a primal condition is the ideal goal he yearns and works for.

Yet for all his external commitments and inner complications, Schiller kept an unbroken faith in art as an influence on human affairs, indeed as one of the main shaping forces in the evolution of mankind. He worked the theme out, aptly enough, in a poem rather than a historical essay; but it dates from the same months of 1789 as his first history lectures, and it shares their characteristic method of reconstructing the distant past as a logical development from imagined beginnings. The poem 'The Artists' (*Die Künstler*—i. 173 ff.) starts with an emblematic figure of eighteenth-century humanity posing serenely at the close of the age, the fortunate product of past developments, quietly confident in his expectations of the future: 'Maturest son of time, / Through reason free and strong through laws . . . / Lord over nature'. But precisely because he is so privileged in the present, he needs to be reminded of his debt to the power that has brought him this far, having found him long ago 'orphaned / On life's barren strand . . . / Prey to wild chance', and set him on the path towards full humanity. Art was that power. It refined his animal nature and his ideas, and it did so by embodying in its beautiful forms the rational truths that mankind would only arrive at much later. Art was the foreplay of reason, the only means by which primitive humanity could absorb to good effect what it was destined one day to know abstractly and with full awareness. 'What we have here perceived as beauty / Will one day come to meet us as the truth.'

This is not yet Keats's belief in a self-sufficient beauty which *is* the truth; but nor is it just the commonplace eighteenth-century notion that the beautiful and the good somehow harmonize by happy coincidence—that vicious actions, for example, repel us because they are ugly. Schiller has turned that vaguely perceived relation of beauty to truth into a historical movement from one to the other, an education of mankind. The 'childish imagination' grasped 'virtue' in symbols before Solon ever formulated a law, and certainly long before 'ageing Reason' devised ethical systems. Art is thus a major part of a 'universal plan'.

Yet this theory, so close to everything Schiller the historian struggled to believe in and to make others believe in, did not quite satisfy Schiller the artist. Could beauty and art really be just the means to necessary abstractions like reason and virtue, the pretty packaging for austere messages? If this were so, then life in humanity's late epochs was going to be *too* austere, since people would have thrown away beauty to live by those abstractions. Such a sequence might suit a philosopher (it was to be the historical argument of Hegel's *Aesthetics*). It might be acceptable in other areas of life: Lessing argued for example that religion was a progressive education of mankind in which crude beliefs gave way to a finer faith till at last people acted ethically for the sake of it—at which point the 'textbooks' of Old and New Testament could be thrown away. But if mankind were likewise to throw away art and beauty, would it any longer *be* mankind, the unique mixture of senses and spirit that we know? A terminus somewhere in abstraction would not so much solve the time-traveller's problems as dissolve the traveller himself. And so the linear progress Schiller's poem argues is suddenly cut across by the idea that art, artists, beauty are still needed, will always be needed. They are not just a means, but an important part of the end, they must be there *at* the end:

> With you, the plant with which spring started,
> Nature began to shape man's soul;
> With you, the garland of the harvest,
> She rounds her labours to a whole.　　(i. 184 f.)

Quite when that will be Schiller does not make clear, but his optimistic tone suggests it will be soon. This is surprising, given the negative image of eighteenth-century society that his youthful plays present. Did things really now seem so rosy at the end of the same decade? Perhaps from the higher viewpoint of history (or the socially more settled one of a professor of history) the civilization of the Age of Reason loomed larger than the local imperfections of German society.

Yet in some moods even the progress achieved by reason in modern times could itself appear negative, part of a historical movement in the wrong direction. 'The Artists' brings back imagination at a late stage in the advance towards rationality; 'The Gods of Greece' (*Die Götter Griechenlands*, 1788), a year earlier, had lamented that whole advance. Imagination in this poem is the *victim* of rationality: imagination once made the world inhabitable, gave warmth and colour and a feeling of divine presence to what modern science now describes with cold sobriety. Where once the sun was Helios driving his chariot across the heavens, 'Soulless now a ball of fire turns'. Modern truth is arid; modern culture, like modern society, looks back to a lost paradise: 'Lovely world, where are you vanished? Will you not come back again, Nature's sweet blossom time?' (Schubert caught the essence of Schiller's long elegy by taking just the stanza containing these words and setting it to one of his most wistful tunes.)

So a longed-for past can devalue the present and call in question the whole idea of progress. More radically still, the sceptical idealist can query the very hope that fuels his idealism. The poem 'Resignation' (*Resignation*, 1786) recognizes that hope has no guarantees; its various props—the idea of justice in another life, a better future, benevolent gods ('Slily dreamt up to save an ailing plan')—will all prove illusory. Hope must be, must have already been, its own reward:

> You had your hopes, there'll be no more accounting,
> Your faith was all the happiness they'll pay.
> You had wise men to ask when you were doubting;
> But once refuse the moment's bounty,
> It's gone for ever and a day.

There is a grim, bourgeois irony in the materialist image: hope is a credit note drawn on the future in recognition that the idealist has sacrificed his immediate happiness, but it may never be honoured. This was written the year before Schiller read Kant on history and was fired by the notion that reality might be transformed by self-fulfilling idealism. That—in itself very provisional—optimism was plainly built over an abyss of doubt.

These swings from grand assertion to negation and doubt may seem extreme: how can a thinker be that volatile? But Schiller is less and more than a thinker, he is a poet. He is often called a 'philosophical poet', but that does not mean he simply uses verse to expound settled doctrines. On the contrary, he responds to ideas with changing emotions as his moods change. Where a professional philosopher would settle for a position before making public utterance, Schiller captures the movement towards a position and between positions, confesses the tension between faith and doubt which is at least as much a reality of the intellectual life seriously lived as any stable 'philosophy' is.

Clearly, though, the issue is not just an internal, psychological one; it also hangs on how the world goes. In the summer of 1789 as Schiller was formulating his more optimistic statements on human rationality and progress, history was building to a crisis that would provide a resounding answer. Or rather two successive answers, as discordant as Schiller's opposed moods.

3 Two crises

The Grand Disillusion

The first answer was that Universal History had achieved the millennium: a century of enlightenment was culminating in social revolution, France was being transformed, the ideal was being made real. If it could happen in that great and long dominant nation, what might not follow elsewhere? Moreover it was happening without bloodshed; history seemed to be changing its nature. That made it indeed, as Wordsworth was later to write, a 'dawn' in which it was 'bliss to be alive', especially for those who were young and had the new age of a realm of reason all before them. Germans shared the enthusiasm of other European onlookers.

But then with regicide and the Reign of Terror, history relapsed into its more familiar ways, confirmed for Germans when the Revolutionary Wars brought armies of distinctly unideal Frenchmen on to their soil. A grand disillusion set in, proportionate to the hopes and expectations that had been raised. And since philosophy and reason had been credited with the new start, they were now blamed for its failure. Benign theory seemed to have led to atrocious acts. The French Revolution marks not so much the culmination as the end of the Enlightenment; it gave Enlightenment and all it stood for a bad name.

Schiller's response to events in France was not so simple. He was not carried away by sudden enthusiasm, but nor did he abjure reason and all its works when things went awry. Instead he probed deeper into the place of reason in human nature and its complex interactions with sense and emotion, to see why it might have failed at this point in history, and to show how the complex mixture which made up mankind might be helped—prepared, educated—to do better one day.

The work in which he did this combines all Schiller's

strengths and all his involvements: the grand overview of his reflective poems and historical essays, the psychological penetration of his dramas, the sharp observation of the social and cultural critic, the interest in pathology of the trained doctor, and (in the teeth of harsh realities) the undaunted Utopian impulse of the idealist. It is also a classic essay in aesthetics which bears the—for revolutionary times—unexpected and provocative title *On the Aesthetic Education of Man* (*Über die ästhetische Erziehung des Menschen*, 1795).

A writer struggling to live by his pen might not have taken on such an ambitious and probably uncommercial project. But Schiller now had an opportune breathing-space. In 1791 admirers at the Copenhagen court, disturbed by a false report of his death, gave him a three-year pension. Schiller wrote the first draft of his *Aesthetic Education* as a series of actual letters to his benefactor Friedrich Christian, Duke of Schleswig-Holstein-Augustenburg; and the final published text keeps to letter form.

As is the way with complex works that grow to meet the demands of their time, the elements came together gradually and unplanned. It is almost as if Schiller was brought to confront the political problem despite himself, compelled by connections he was not at first clearly aware of. There is little direct mention of the French Revolution in his other correspondence, which is surprising, since it fitted perfectly his teleological vision and his rational hopes for history. Körner asks his opinion of it without even getting a reply (24 Oct./10 Nov. 1789). Later, when they both speak of 'the good cause' (Körner 24 Feb./ Schiller 21 Dec. 1792), they do not mean revolution but individual liberty and freedom of expression, which need protecting as much from revolutionary as from absolutist power. They are prepared to use the Revolution as a stalking-horse so as to put their liberal principles across. Schiller suggests (6 Nov. 1792) that Körner should write an essay on Cromwell: it is a good time for a 'healthy profession of faith about revolutions'. An account of Cromwell, he thinks, will seem to favour opponents of revolution, and make it possible to utter home truths of the kind absolutist governments should be told. That was also one intention behind Schiller's planned appeal to the French people on behalf of the threatened Louis XVI (21 Dec. 1792). It sounds as if

Schiller is still the constitutional monarchist who wrote Posa's speeches in the audience scene of *Don Carlos*.

Before the appeal could be written, Louis had been executed. Schiller, who had been following every political move closely in the *Moniteur*, was too sickened even to read a French newspaper (to Körner, 4 Feb. 1793). Instead he threw his energies into a very different project, an essay on Beauty first mentioned in the same letter with the royal pamphlet. This looks like escapism— aesthetics as the furthest possible remove from politics. Yet the aesthetic theorizing seems unable to get away from politics, as if there were some subterranean relation between them. Political concepts and metaphors keep cropping up. The *Kallias Letters* written to Körner in 1793 speak revealingly of 'those of us for whom freedom is the highest principle' (v. 407) and throughout this first attempt to explain the phenomenon of beauty Schiller works with the ideas of freedom and compulsion as they appear in nature and art. He defines beauty as 'freedom in appearance' (*Freiheit in der Erscheinung*)—i.e. freedom as manifested in the sensuous world of appearance, but also (punningly) freedom in appearance only, because in reality everything that exists must be shaped by natural forces and purposes. Beauty can occur only when these pressures do not show up obtrusively. The form can then seem to be an end in itself, not serving any alien purpose or bearing any yoke of servitude; it is in a state of 'self-determination made visible' (v. 401). Viewed aesthetically, 'every natural phenomenon is a free citizen, with the same rights as the most noble, and may not be *compelled* even for the sake of the whole, but absolutely must *consent* to everything' (v. 421). The political metaphor, with its topical reference to a tyrannical Rousseauian 'volonté générale', strengthens the claims of aesthetics to be relevant to life: 'beauty in the sensuous world' can be 'the happy symbol of how life in the moral world should be lived' (v. 425).

Similar connections are made in *Grace and Dignity* (*Über Anmut und Würde*, also 1793). The new essay goes on from static beauty to beauty in motion and, more generally, to the different ways morality is physically manifested in human behaviour. Grace is an ideal balance of sensuous and moral in our responses to situations. But what shapes our movements and gestures is a permanent set of mind or character (*Gesinnung*) deeper than deliberate acts of moral control (these would be unlikely to result in graceful movement). Informed but not inhibited by a governing ethos, movements can feel free to the agent and appear free (and hence beautiful) to the observer. The analogy Schiller offers for this is 'a monarchy so administered that, although everything runs in accordance with a single will, the individual citizen can persuade himself that he is living in his own way and merely obeying his own inclination' (v. 460). Political terms can also graphically illustrate a wrong balance between the individual's sensuous and moral nature: too tight a control and government ceases to be liberal, too lax a hand and it ceases to be government. Moral rigorism is like 'a monarchy where too strict a surveillance by the ruler checks every free impulse'; unchecked sensuality is like 'a wild ochlocracy [mob rule] where the citizen, in refusing to obey the rightful ruler, does not become free, but merely falls under the brutal despotism of the lower classes' (v. 463). This last twist of the metaphor had an obvious topicality in 1793.

If images of ruling and rulers, power and repression, legislation and constitution, are so central to Schiller's essays, politics must have been as much on his mind as aesthetics. It is true that parallels between the workings of the individual and of the state go back to Aristotle; but they are not pressed so far nor do they show anything like Schiller's passionate interest in the politics of mind-and-matter or the psycho-physiology of the body politic. To say the least, in using politics to throw light on aesthetics he was throwing as much light back on politics, and exploring the issues of the day at one remove. He was also developing a theory that could operate equally at the level of macro- and micro-processes, analyse phenomena and activities at all levels into the same human constants, and read off the deviations from an always precarious balance. So that when later the *Aesthetic Letters* treat the Revolution directly, it is not farfetched but an obvious reciprocal metaphor to call the creation of a true political freedom 'the most perfect of all works of art' (v. 572). Indeed it is barely a metaphor any longer. For by now Schiller has drawn the logical conclusion of his anthropological approach, namely that activities which have fundamentals in common can also act upon each other. Art can affect politics. Hence the at first sight bizarre proposal that 'in order to solve the political problem in practice, we must go via the aesthetic problem, because it is through beauty that we pass to freedom' (v. 573).

There is a distant echo here of the familiar eighteenth-century idea that 'taste' is a factor in behaviour—distant, because Schiller has gone much deeper into why that is so. He has also taken the notion out of its normal gentlemanly sphere and applied it to popular entertainment: 'Drive out what is gratuitous, frivolous and crude from their pleasures and you will gradually banish it from their actions . . . Surround them with symbols of what is good, until appearance overcomes reality and art overcomes nature' (v. 596). He is concerned with all classes of society because in their different ways they have all failed to seize their chance in the historic moment of the Revolution: 'a *physical* possibility seems given . . . to make true freedom the basis of political association. Vain hope! The *moral* possibility is lacking, and the generous moment finds an unreceptive [in the first draft 'a corrupt'] generation' (v. 580). In other words, Schiller is explaining the Revolution's failures by the human factor—this at a time when Robespierre was claiming that 'the French seem to have a two-thousand-year start on the rest of humanity; it is tempting to regard them as a separate species.'

But in place of moral lament or polemic, Schiller explains the human failure in turn by the whole development of mankind from the legendary individual harmony and social cohesion of the Greeks down to the specialization and divided labour through which modern society denies such wholeness to all its members. True, the species may have benefited from some specialized achievements, yet even there the individual in question has lost—and what shall it profit a man to achieve some narrow purpose and 'lose his own self' (*Sich selbst versäumen*—v. 588)? The fragmented beings of modern Europe (later theories would speak of their 'alienation') have suffered precisely this loss. Professionally they are the creatures of their set tasks; psychologically they are out of balance, too much mind or too much sense; socially they are either 'savages' (the lower classes) or 'barbarians' (the lax and decadent cultivated classes)—these last capable in the extreme case, as a related essay says, of 'pursuing an ideal of political happiness through all the atrocities of anarchy' (v. 692). Disharmonious in themselves, such people could hardly pass peacefully from one kind of social organization to a radically different one. This was not a failure of Reason. Men simply lacked the integration and mature adaptability which would have allowed them to exercise it.

So it seems as if the serene progression from beauty to truth which Schiller sketched in his poem 'The Artists' never really happened after all; it was an ideal. But for Schiller that means not that it must be abandoned, but that it must become the prescription for a new start. It cannot of course be an instant cure for the ills in which a long historical development has come to grief—that is avowedly 'a task for more than one century' (v. 590). History, Sisyphus-like, simply has to begin again, with the artist once more as its guide and ally, and with beauty and art constituting the only possible 'third character' (v. 576) that can mediate between warring human elements.

Yet if society is corrupt and fragmented, the classes polarized, men's senses split off from reason, how can art—itself one of society's products—ever escape being shaped by these ills in order to have a healing influence? History records that art has often simply shared the faults of its age. Schiller knows this, he is not starry-eyed; but he argues undaunted that even if art has never freed itself from the taints of its time before, that is still what it has to do now. It was never in any case the fault of 'Art' in the abstract, but of *artists*. It is their responsibility to stand back from their age, find an independent voice deep within themselves or in some better time (for example Greece), and then give their age what it needs—which may not be what it wants.

For this they have an aptly versatile medium. Beauty is dual, sense and spirit, just as human nature is dual; it therefore contains and can provide whatever we need when we need it. It can invigorate or soothe; it can stimulate our urge for 'form' (*Formtrieb*), i.e. the impulse to order experience; it can satisfy our appetite for 'life', i.e. the impulse to absorb the world's sensuous reality (*Stofftrieb*). In ideal conditions art would fuse these two fundamental objects, 'form' and 'life', into a single perfectly integrated object, 'living shape' (*lebende Gestalt*)—and this is Schiller's definition of beauty, the culmination of his theoretical aesthetics. In such ideal conditions, a corresponding integration of our 'formal' and 'material' impulses would occur and generate a third, the 'play impulse' (*Spieltrieb*) (v. 614). This would mean total liberation from the pressures and purposes of everyday so that we could relive and savour objects, emotions and ideas to the full. They would all be drawn from actual experience, but instead of being used and discarded (that is, in essence neglected) as they are in practical living, they would be presented for their own sake. This would be the material—made 'real' in a new sense through being detached from everyday reality—out of which the artist creates a work; and the responsive reader or spectator would correspondingly perceive that material as newly realized in this sense. To help them respond, moreover, these recipients have their own analogous stock of experience waiting to be redisposed according to the formal patterns the artist has created; waiting, that is, to realize the work of art itself which without that imaginative input is only potential, not actual. This is probably what Schiller means when he describes the individual mind as in a state not of 'mere indeterminacy' but of 'limitless determinability'; it is not an empty *tabula rasa*, it has an accumulated store of reality that is ready to be reshaped (v. 634). That readiness is as important as the material itself, because it implies an openness to the alternative patterns created by other minds which makes art a liberating and liberalizing force. As Körner had suggested, the pleasure in beauty lies in the sympathy we feel with the objects we contemplate; it inspires us to widen our own bounds (4 Feb. 1793).

It is then not just the objects and experiences represented, but also the faculties with which we respond to them in the enjoyment of art that are thereby restored to their full value and range: restored from the effect of specialized work, stultifying habit, narrow personal or social horizons. This double restitution, of the phenomenal world and of the human observer, but particularly the second, is the point of Schiller's central aphorism in the fifteenth of the *Aesthetic Letters*: 'Human beings only play when they are in the full sense of the word human, and *they are only fully human when they play'* (v. 618; italics in the text). Schiller has taken Kant's pioneering but essentially negative definition of aesthetic experience as 'pleasure without any practical interest' and given it a positive substance and dynamism. The mere abstention from practical demands which Kant envisaged did very much suggest a *tabula rasa*, a complete withdrawal from the patterns of life as we know it. Schiller has turned this into the activity of play with the rich resources of experience.

Although such totally free play is an ideal condition, Schiller clearly assumes that all actual aesthetic experience gets somewhere near it, and does so to some worthwhile purpose. Hence his confidence that the principle he has declared in that central aphorism 'will carry, I promise you, the whole structure of aesthetic art and of the yet more difficult art of life' (v. 618); that is, through the practical effect which aesthetic experience, so defined, is capable of bringing about.

But what *is* the effect of aesthetic experience, that such practical claims can be made for it? The answer is, nil—for any immediate purpose. Yet precisely this is the gain; for raised to a free but not vacuous contemplation of experience, with the sense-spirit balance restored, human beings will be able to make a fresh start (v. 635 f.). This is a beneficial larger version of something Schiller finds in our everyday micro-processes, namely a quasi-aesthetic 'free' moment that intervenes between any perception or thought and the ensuing willed action. And the fresh start must be, axiomatically for Schiller with his Enlightenment faith in nature and her ultimately benevolent designs for mankind, a start in a good direction. Balance restored means primal innocence restored. Beauty (as 'The Artists' argued) embodies and anticipates truth; the experience of beauty cannot lead us astray.

Finally, again as in that poem, art is not just a stage and a means on the way to a rational goal; aesthetic freedom is also the ideal condition Schiller prophesies when action has achieved the political millennium. The harmonies of a free society will be akin to those of art, an aesthetic version of what Kant called the 'kingdom of ends', where no one is reduced to serving as someone else's means but all are valued and respected in and for themselves. Aesthetics becomes the ethics of the future.

Did all this really speak to the revolutionary times? Not immediately, since it is expressly a long-term proposal. For that reason it cannot fairly be ridiculed as unpractical and inadequate to the moment. Some have thought that even in the long term Schiller merely serves the cause of reaction by wanting mankind first perfected before society's institutions are changed. Kant by contrast had argued that freedom should be learned in the practice of freedom. Yet the point is that an attempt had just been made to change institutions, with some grim effects. What is more, observers on the spot in Paris traced these effects to failings that closely matched Schiller's analysis: passions overcoming judgement, a converse tyranny of reason without feeling, insight not supported by strength or courage, energy harnessed to ignorance. There was room for Schiller's conception of a necessary human wholeness at least as a supplement, if not an alternative, to other attempts at progress; for he nowhere actually demands a moratorium on social change. But he does argue that a deeper human transformation is the best hope of making change beneficial and lasting. Earlier he had admired Mirabeau for planning, while the new French constitution was still in the making, an educational system that would give it 'eternal duration' (to Körner, 15 Oct. 1792). Under absolutism it had been vital to educate and enlighten the ruler. In this new age of mass politics, it was vital to educate everyone. Revolutions in themselves guaranteed nothing; as Kant had said five years before the French specimen, they only exchanged one despot for another and replaced old prejudices with a new set. There was reason to work on the human material of history.

The *Aesthetic Letters* are both complex and simple, and in more than one way. First, they are complex in doing two things at once, theorizing about beauty and prescribing for mankind's ills. Yet they are simple in finally uniting those two things, linking aesthetics and politics at the subterranean level Schiller had for some time divined. The revolutionary crisis taught him how deep, in every sense, his faith in art was. Then the *Letters* are also complex to read. They move in successive waves of analysis, each seemingly more intricate and abstract than the last. Sometimes Schiller apologizes for the unrelenting abstraction, but otherwise he makes no concessions (as contemporaries were quick to complain). The reader is bombarded with antithetical concepts, has to follow their connections, their kaleidoscopically shifting mutual relations, their promised reconciliations. It is easy to boggle. Yet paradoxically the text can and should be read for its simple structures—read fast, and with no brooding over the precise sense of every term, taking each rather as a brushstroke that builds up a bold picture, a variation on a persistent theme. If one reads thus so to speak from the whole to the parts, then concepts and combinations all fall into place as restating, in what is itself high philosophic play, the dividedness of human nature in every sphere and the need to heal division for the sake of individual happiness and the good of society. Parts of that message were already present long before, in *The Effects of Theatre on the People* and in 'The Artists'. Making the message systematic was not just an emulation of Kant, to whose three Critiques Schiller by now owed a great deal. It was a necessary act of self-reaffirmation. Where the Revolution had driven many people to doubt their enlightened principles, it drove Schiller to lay—or lay bare—deeper foundations for his, and to face the long task of building on them for a future second chance.

'This man, this Goethe . . .'

Another kind of reaffirmation was also needed. The political crisis of the Revolution had broken in on an existing personal crisis. Since his problems with *Don Carlos*, Schiller had been working his way through the thickets of theory towards (he hoped) the open ground of a new poetic practice. Restoring confidence in his own creativity was not just a technical but an existential necessity: he had shaped his life and risked everything on the assumption that he was truly a poet, and potentially a great one. His current work had its literary qualities —both in historical narrative and philosophical argument, his prose style is clear, thrusting, often rhetorically majestic. But these were not the things he really wanted to write. Aesthetics was mainly a means to an end, even if the *Aesthetic Letters* did turn out to be 'the best thing I have done in my life' (to Hoven,

21 Nov. 1794); as for history, the only thing that still gripped him in his work on the Thirty Years War was a figure whose fate cried out to be treated in the freer and richer mode of drama: the Emperor's general, Wallenstein.

Since the move to Jena there was also a new difficulty, seemingly trivial yet real. Goethe was now only a stone's throw away in Weimar, and to have that immense talent so near was all the more of a reproach to Schiller's dormant poetic powers. His reactions when they met were negative. He found Goethe altogether too cool and self-contained: he could captivate people, especially with stories about Italy where he had just spent two invigorating years of freedom; but he lacked all effusiveness, he seemed as distant as a god, the perfect egoist; they could never be close (to Körner, 12 Sept. 1788, 2 Feb. 1789). Yet Goethe's personality was too compelling to be ignored. Schiller's feelings were a violent mixture, 'not unlike what Brutus and Cassius must have felt for Caesar. I could murder his spirit and love him again from my heart'; and, from darker psychic levels than such literary allusion: 'I regard him as a haughty prude who must be got with child and humiliated before the world' (to Körner, 2 Feb. 1789). This was love-hate with a vengeance, and poetic rivalry, resentment and self-assertion were at its root. For 'this man, this Goethe, is simply in my way . . . How easily *his* genius was carried along by his destiny, and how I have had to struggle right up to the present moment!' (to Körner, 9 March 1789). Whatever Schiller said, it was Goethe's recognition he plainly wanted more than anyone else's—recognition of his own different poetic claims, his difficulties, his achievements. Years later, privileged to watch a new work of Goethe's growing, he could declare that 'in the face of excellence there is no freedom but love' (to Goethe, 2 July 1796). But by then he was not just recognized, he was accepted as a friend and literary partner.

Goethe had equal and opposite reservations about Schiller, largely because of the wild effusiveness of his early works, a quality which—ten years older, and now classically enlightened by Italy—Goethe had purged from his own work. He too believed there could be no point of contact between them, they were 'spiritual antipodes'. But a chance meeting (it is possible

Schiller engineered it) after a lecture at the Jena Scientific Society led to a long talk at Schiller's house. This revealed a surprising area of agreement between them, even though they started from opposite principles: if they were antipodes, it was of a single intellectual globe. What they had reacted against in each other was typological divergence, and the types complemented each other when seen from a higher standpoint.

Schiller, taking that standpoint and his historic opportunity, sent Goethe a remarkable letter (23 Aug. 1794) which is at once the minutes of their Jena conversation, a piece of literary diplomacy, and the first sketch for his last and most imaginative major essay, *On Naïve and Reflective Poetry* (*Über naive und sentimentalische Dichtung*, 1795). The letter distinguishes an 'intuitive' and a 'speculative' mind, the one proceeding from the variety of experience, the other from the unity of ideas. But neither, if truly creative, stays static: the intuitive mind moves from a grasp of particulars towards underlying laws, the speculative moves from abstract generalizations towards their real embodiments. The common ground they share is the path they are both following—from opposite ends. They are bound to meet halfway. In Jena they had.

Schiller's letter arrived in time for Goethe's forty-fifth birthday, an astonishing present. 'Your letter', Goethe replied, 'sums up my existence and urges me on to a more active and enterprising use of my powers' (27 Aug. 1794). Their meeting and this exchange of letters mark the start of a ten-year partnership, which was to bear out in practice Schiller's belief in the fruitful reconciliations that are possible beyond —indeed, latent in—antitheses.

Building a theory of reciprocity and interdependence around Goethe and himself rescued Schiller from resentments and self-doubt. It meant his creative difficulties were no longer a chance affliction, to be shamed by Goethe's imperturbable productiveness; it was simply his different nature to theorize his way towards the concrete realities poetry needed; he must after all have been wrong to think he had ever enjoyed a carefree spontaneity of expression (to Körner, 25 May 1792). Goethe was no longer a living reproach, but a beacon on the necessary path. What once seemed his excessive involvement in the real—'his way of seeing is too sensuous and *handles* things too much for my liking', Schiller had once protested (to Körner, 1 Nov. 1790)—was now the thing that made him exemplary. It is because he is the modern poet who 'perhaps departs least from the sensuous truth of things' (v. 738) that Goethe joins Shakespeare and the Greeks as Schiller's literary Ideal.

These were not just standard great names, accepted for conventional reasons. In the essay *On Naïve and Reflective Poetry*, Schiller grounds their greatness in a theory that gives his typological conceptions a larger historical frame. Perceptually and poetically, the Greeks were the unspoiled children of the race. They could render the natural world fully and unself-consciously because they were still part of it, they did not suffer from the inner divisions of later ages. They created perfect forms from a vision that was whole, even if (indeed because) it was limited. But then came the cultural Fall of mankind. The rise of more complex social organization, the victory of Christian religion with its elaborate and often perverse spirituality working against the grain of nature, the dominance of dualistic philosophies which were the secular sequel to Christianity—all these things cut human beings off from the roots of a simpler unitary nature. Awareness of this separation only enhanced it, and created a new entity—not to say a goddess—never known to the Greeks: 'The Greeks had natural feeling; we have a feeling for nature' (v. 711).

The poetic consequence of this is that the modern writer will never give us 'the object itself'(v. 731), but only the thoughts and emotions it arouses. His reflective consciousness is interposed like a veil between him and the world of things. Even when his own emotions are the theme, they will tend to be reflexive, observed and commentated rather than simply expressed (v. 731 f.). All this, it is true, makes modern writing richer and more complex; moderns can look back like sophisticated adults at that Greek childhood and find it 'naïve'. Yet this term is positive not dismissive, because no amount of modern sophistication can make up for our loss of naturalness, integration, immediacy of vision. We can only admire and wonder at those rare writers—Shakespeare, Molière, Cervantes, and now Goethe—whose individual genius transcends their location in modernity and who seem, in their unscathed naturalness, like some miraculous outcrop of the oldest rock-layers of literature. The rest of modern writing can only aspire to regain that lost state, and recreate a new wholeness of vision and perfection of form. The awareness of lost naturalness and the impulse to restore it together make modern writing 'reflective', what Schiller calls 'sentimentalisch'—again, not a dismissive term, since it is not the ordinary German word for 'sentimental' and Schiller is concerned with an anything but shallow or trite emotion.

Restoring and recreating wholeness does not mean going back. There *is* no going back to earlier simplicities. Rousseau himself, whose ideas of primal innocence and social corruption clearly lie behind Schiller's, is invoked expressly so that Schiller can reject that opinion, which he wrongly thinks Rousseau favoured (v. 730 f.). The aim is a new simplicity beyond complexity, not a retreat from but an embracing and harmonizing of modern discord such as would give real sense to the vacuous term 'post-modern'. Yet so great are the complexity and discords of modern culture that this must seem an impossible task. Schiller none the less has a vision—perhaps one should say a mirage—of the ideal poetic work that would achieve it, or at least of how such a work would feel to the reader. It would hold in balance richness and simplicity, energy and tranquillity, stasis and movement; it would express the full potential of human thought and feeling, and yet still give this infinite content a concrete, finite form; it would resolve all conflict between Reality and the Ideal (v. 751). He calls this ultimate poetic work an 'idyll', though it is something quite different from the regressive pastoral pictures the term usually denotes. Schiller borrows the name as a sign that, against all the odds, a poem of this kind would make real the serenity which in conventional idylls is only an escapist illusion. For a time he actively plans to write one himself—or rather, to write *it*: for what other work would be left for poets to create if this were once accomplished? It would be the triumph of modern over naïve poetry. Aptly, its subject was to be the apotheosis of Hercules, the transition from earth to Olympus, the transformation of Man into God (to Humboldt, 30 Nov. 1795).

Short of such an achievement of the poetic millennium, all 'reflective' writing—and this, for historical and critical purposes, is the most important part of Schiller's argument—is meantime necessarily in the elegiac mode, for its theme is always in the last analysis the gap between present reality and the lost natural ideal. The individual work may be an elegy in the narrower sense, a lament for what has been lost; or it may be a satire, humorous or savage, on what is all too painfully present; or it may be an idyll of the traditional sort evoking before our eyes the happy state before the Fall. All these are not so much the external sub-genres the words 'elegy', 'satire' and 'idyll' normally refer to, but the available 'modes of feeling' (v. 721, 745) the possible variations on a basic attitude from which the modern writer cannot escape.

Schiller's few and seemingly simple categories prove to be illuminating and exhaustive but also flexible in practical use, as he shows in the compressed survey of eighteenth-century writing, not just German, which is part of the essay. His historical-cum-typological theory serves to place writers, his 'modes of feeling' narrow the focus, and his concept of an ideal sense–spirit balance helps to gauge how far abstract ideas—from which, on his analysis, modern literature must necessarily spring—have been integrated with percepts, i.e. have actually become poetry. He also demands an ultimate seriousness of feeling in the 'play' of art. Beside the humour of Fielding, Sterne, and Wieland, Voltaire's satire seems too unserious and unfeeling, even for mockery (v. 726 f.). The earnestness of Rousseau, in contrast, never descends to frivolity but nor does it ever rise to truly poetic play (v. 730). Klopstock and Haller move the reader by ideas not objects, they are more didactic than representational; like James Thomson's in *The Seasons*, their poetry is musical but not concrete, and thus falls short of the 'living shape' which was the ideal of beauty established in the *Aesthetic Letters* (v. 731–5). As for the poetry of Ossian, at this date not finally revealed as modern pastiche, it is unambiguously in the 'reflective' mode, which already hints that it is not the genuine ancient article it purported to be (v. 730). Schiller called his mini-essay in practical criticism 'Judgement Day' (to Goethe, 23 Nov. 1795). It is an apt description, since his assessments of writers are uncompromising but just and based on coherent principles. They also temper justice with mercy by recognizing that a modern writer—unlike his 'naïve' ancestor, who could complete to perfection a limited project—is attempting, and is given moral credit for attempting, an infinite task.

On Naïve and Reflective Poetry presents us with the now familiar myth of original innocence and ancient Greek wholeness; but when transplanted to the soil of literature, it becomes more concrete and hence checkable. Where the ideal Greek society is past and cannot be directly inspected, the ancient texts can be reread to test for the qualities Schiller credits them with and for the effects they are supposed to have on the modern reader. The result may be sceptical questions. Is there an absolute break between naïve and reflective poetry? Are there not limits to how limited the self-consciousness of *any* creative writer can be? Is *all* ancient nature description, for example in the lyrical choruses of Greek tragedy, really different in kind from its modern counterpart? Yet what matters most for practical purposes is the light Schiller's argument throws on the relationship between the poetic mind and the world, and on its different possible modalities. If his setting up of modern writers as agents of cultural restoration seems ambitious beyond either the needs or the reach of poetry, and itself something of a period piece, still it is not hard to make out behind it a more familiar and timeless concern of literature. For when Schiller evokes a form of expression 'where the sign wholly vanishes in the thing signified' (v. 706), or when he looks back to a kind of writing that was 'the most complete possible imitation of the real' (v. 717), or when he celebrates Goethe as the poet who in their day has come 'nearest to the sensuous reality of things' (v. 738), he is formulating an aim that is perennial in Western writing. 'Realism' was not yet a term of literary criticism in the eighteenth century, but in these phrases of Schiller's it seems on the point of being born. Indeed, when he says of the naïve writer, wholly possessed by the object, that he 'stands behind his work like God behind the created universe' (v. 713), he is anticipating almost to the word the idea of modern realism as an escape from gratuitous subjectivity that Flaubert was to formulate—also, incidentally, with the Greeks in mind—in the next century (letter to Louise Colet, 9 Dec. 1852). So that if the conception of the naïve was a myth, it was a potentially fruitful one for eighteenth-century writing, and for Schiller's own. It directed attention to the object, and away from the abstract reflection and self-sufficient feeling that the age and its poetry were addicted to. It was one more practical prescription of the critic as doctor.

Schiller's essay contains further intricacies and apparent inconsistencies that have been much argued over. But its main arguments are strong and intuitively persuasive. They entail answers to other central questions about literature, including how to distinguish sexual frankness from pornography (v. 724 f.), and how to avoid pitching the claims of culture too high, as purely moral 'uplift', or too low, as mere mindless 'relaxation' (v. 764 f.). Above all they give a plausible shape to the history of European poetic sensibility from Homer to Schiller's own day—and indeed beyond. For in raising to the surface the most general emotional pressure that shaped all modern writing, Schiller was diagnosing in advance its most dramatic expression yet, the European Romantic movement that was stirring into life as he wrote.

In fact, Goethe was to say in 1830 that the very 'conception of Classical and Romantic poetry now causing so much conflict and division' went back to the differences between himself and Schiller, and to the essay Schiller had written 'to defend himself against me'. That does justice to the essay's seminal quality, but not to its higher historical perspective or to the eirenic conception of literature that superseded the old European 'quarrel between ancient and modern'. Nor, above all, does it do justice to Schiller's dream of one day rehousing the spirit in an adequate objective form, which sets him clearly apart from Romantic subjectivism and justifies his title as Goethe's 'Classical' partner. Self-defence and self-assertion may have been the roots of *On Naïve and Reflective Poetry*, but the finished work rises above self to affirm difference and the common purpose which difference paradoxically implies. Schiller yearned not just to be recognized for what he was, but to transcend what he was. That yearning shows up in his language, which by now has practically outgrown Kant's influence and the ambition to be rigorously philosophical. Instead of aiming at austere abstraction, the writing now has a tone of frank, if contained, emotion. This makes the essay itself as moving an elegy as any to the lost and future ideal it treats.

4 Defeat and victory

'How it really was'

Schiller's new and grandest work and the centrepiece of his literary career, the trilogy *Wallenstein* (1800), bears the marks of both those crises. The French Revolution had changed his view of history; the urge to emulate—for personal and for broader cultural reasons—Goethe's kind of poetry changed his art. The two things came together to produce an impressive new sobriety.

The changed historical vision is put bleakly in an essay probably of the late 1790s. History offers a scene 'where mad chance appears to reign rather than a wise plan . . . The world, as a historical object, is at root nothing but the conflict of natural forces with each other and with human freedom, and the outcome is what history reports' (v. 802 f.). The odds, in the physical realm at least, are stacked against that puny 'human freedom'.

The changed art already shows in the way Schiller was going about his new project. He was managing, he wrote, 'to keep the subject-matter outside myself and give only the object'—something only the naïve poets were supposed to be able to do—and he was working not in feverish identification but coolly, with 'the pure love of the artist' (to Goethe, 28 Nov. 1796). He was helped in this by the new kind of character he had chosen as his central figure: Wallenstein, the Catholic Emperor's general in the Thirty Years War, was no youthful idealist, but a hardened soldier, a realist, perhaps even a *Realpolitiker*, if in the end a failed one. He was not the type to inspire Schiller's old enthusiasm by being martyr to some great cause that was destined eventually to triumph. It is true that he claims to be pursuing the goal of peace (P 1177 ff., D 1949 ff.); but too much uncertainty veils his real intentions, in this as in everything else. Perhaps they are not even firm in his own mind. He has had secret negotiations with the Emperor's Protestant enemies, the Swedes and the Saxons. Is this a prelude to action—the betrayal of the Catholic cause? Is he really out to impose a settlement on an obstinate Austria? And if so, is it with an eye to the public good, or an eye on the Bohemian crown for himself? Or is all of it just an insurance policy against being deposed—as he once was before, only to be called back in dire emergency as the one man with the charisma (and the private means) to raise a new army from nowhere and save Austria from disaster? Precisely this last achievement is what makes him suspect to the court at Vienna: the army is very much Wallenstein's own, a state-within-a-state out of imperial control; the mercenaries are held together in a kind of surrogate nation by loyalty to their general and the dependence of their worldly fortunes on his.

Schiller boldly puts this power-base and precondition of the action before us in the eleven-scene prelude set in Wallenstein's camp (*Wallensteins Lager*), a review of rank-and-file humanity that is designed to draw us into the world of the Thirty Years War and to catch the army's mood and morale before the plot proper unfolds. Nothing could make Schiller's commitment to an 'objective' mode plainer than this attempt at the common touch, which looks back via the crowd scenes of Goethe's *Egmont* which he so admired to those of Shakespeare's *Julius Caesar* (v. 938 f.). The *Camp* is a remarkable performance from a poet with so little natural taste for random common experience. Its figures may be not quite crude enough to be really soldiers, while being too crude to be really Schiller; but the doggerel verse is a striking attempt to bridge the gap, in clear emulation of Goethe's virtuosity in the 1790 *Faust* fragment. And the exposition is unforced and cumulatively clear: this army looks ready to follow Wallenstein when he goes over to the Swedes—when he decides, eventually, that the time is ripe—*if* he ever decides . . . For perhaps he simply enjoys the feeling that he always *could* do so and avenge the Emperor's past slights if he wanted to: 'It gives me pleasure just to feel my power; / But whether I shall *use* it, *that*, I fancy, / Is something *you* can no more tell than anyone' (P 868 ff.)—this to his close associate Terzky who urges him, not for the first time, to act at once. The reason, or pretext, for delaying is Wallenstein's faith in the stars; he will act when they dictate, not sooner. Vainly his generals tell him his fate is not in the stars but in his own mind and hands, that 'your unlucky star, / The only one can damage you, is *doubt*' (P 959 ff.). They are right to sense the tide of opportunity ebbing. Wallenstein's most trusted comrade, Octavio Piccolomini, is intriguing against him, in secret league with the Vienna court which mistrusts its autocratic general and fears the power it was forced to put in his hands.

But precisely this mistrust, which Wallenstein's wife has observed in Vienna, is what drives him towards actual betrayal: 'Oh! they are forcing me, / Pushing me into it against my will' (P 701 f.). When Wallenstein's messenger to the Swedes is intercepted, the mistrust seems justified, the case against him proved. Now he has no choice but to act. Yet how far was he truly guilty? What is certain—perhaps the one thing certain in the whole situation—is that each side has pressed matters towards the end it feared by taking measures to prevent it. That classic political effect is one of the play's great and subtle themes. Schiller in mid-composition called it, half-despairingly, an 'invisible, abstract subject' (to Körner, 28 Nov. 1796). And so it is, beside the more concrete situations of other tragedies. That is what makes it one of the most sophisticated of modern dramas: intentions, precautions, appearances, interpretations, consequences make up a set of 'natural forces' whose complex interplay slowly shapes and then suddenly precipitates the tragic outcome.

The complexity, confusion even (though the situation unfolds, each time one re-reads the play, with masterly clarity) is the measure of Schiller's advance as a dramatist. His first three plays had embodied black-and-white issues in figures that, despite some psychological intricacies, were grandly noble or caricaturally evil. Then in *Don Carlos* the historic issues remained clear, though the villains now got a say, speaking with their own voices. But in *Wallenstein* not even the issues are clear. When Wallenstein and a court emissary swap charge and counter-charge, each seems right while he speaks. So do Wallenstein's false friend Octavio and his passionate admirer Max Piccolomini, when they argue the case between covert cunning and straight dealing. The ethics of Octavio, dutifully betraying the betrayer, are endlessly debatable; and it is not clear whether Schiller presents him as judged or wronged by the worldly reward which is tossed to him for services rendered as the final curtain comes down. Above all we are never sure what Wallenstein's real motives were. We can never know how far he would have gone if left a free hand, precisely because he is not. His hand is forced by events, and that anticipates resolution, in both senses. What dominates his great soliloquy, certainly, is not remorse for real guilt, but a horrified recognition that a play with possibilities has hardened into an imprisoning reality:

> Can it be true? Are all my options closed?
> Retreat impossible if I should choose?
> Must I *perform* the thing I merely *thought*?

He now sees only

> Trackless terrain behind me, and a wall
> Built of my own actions towering up
> To block retreat.   (D 139 ff., 156 f.)

This is the play's other main theme, seemingly just as 'invisible and abstract', but intensely real: there is no such thing as inaction or innocent possibility, planning and temporizing are a kind of action too, generating ample nemesis from a minimum of hubris. For Wallenstein fails. He plays out his historic role of traitor too late: Octavio has undermined his support among the generals, and the common soldiers prove to be more scrupulous over switching sides than seemed likely.

That 'historic role' of Wallenstein's was what first intrigued Schiller. As a historian of the Thirty Years War he had gone along with the conventional view of a man out for revenge on the Emperor, negotiating seriously with the enemy, but delaying too long so that finally he 'did not fall because he rebelled, but rebelled because he fell' (iv. 490 f., 598 ff., 688). Yet there was no historical document to prove that view; and the sources Schiller had used were hardly disinterested—the Catholic party that intrigued against Wallenstein living had written the history when he was dead (iv. 688). So Wallenstein's guilt was not an indisputable fact. On the other hand, there was no document to disprove it either; and history was not the medium for pure counter-speculation.

Drama however offered the scope for just that: speculation could there become imaginative re-enactment, Wallenstein could be rescued from the pro and contra of partisan accounts through artistic empathy. That is what Schiller promises in his Prologue:

> Art shall now bring the human being close
> So you can see, so you can feel his fate.
> That is art's way—to limit, link, and bring
> Extremities back to the ground of nature.   [102 ff.]

This echoes Aristotle's famous statement in the *Poetics* that poetry gets closer to the essential truth than history, which is restricted to what is documentable, contingent, and at best only part of the story. Yet Schiller could hardly have guessed how remarkably his *Wallenstein* would confirm Aristotle's view. For what has become known from documents accessible only long after Schiller's day bears out precisely the subtler, morally ambiguous picture of Wallenstein which the drama gives: the mixed motives, the concern for peace crossed with personal ambition, the trauma of the first dismissal, the indecisiveness, the reluctance to commit himself—not to mention the more predictable haste with which his one-time supporters deserted and disowned him. Art intuited nature, and historiography has now followed in the footsteps of art. In pursuing 'the object itself' for his own poetic reasons and no longer with any thought of reading hopeful patterns in the past, Schiller had managed to meet Ranke's celebrated requirement of the historian and 'show how it really was'.

Wallenstein the man was not just quite unlike Schiller's earlier dramatic characters (except for the ubiquitous element of intrigue or rebellion). He was also wholly out of line with the theory of tragedy that Schiller had evolved in his artistically fallow years. Paradoxically, his masterpiece obeys its own rules, not his. Schiller, the theorist, now argued that tragedy was a balance of suffering and freedom: physical suffering, loss, the destruction of life or happiness on the one hand, and on the other a conscious response by which the tragic figure affirms its deepest commitment, and through that the principle of human autonomy itself. To rise to these heights took a special kind of character, one accustomed to reflecting, resolving, and renouncing, and one for whom there could be more important things than success or even survival. The last section of the essay *On Naïve and Reflective Poetry* sketched this character-type and called it the 'Idealist', not in the sense of having noble ideals (though that was likely as a by-product) but in the formal sense of leading a conscious life rather than the unthinking, instinctive life of its opposite, the Realist. Wallenstein the Realist was thus typologically excluded from tragedy in his author's sense. When he reflects on the morality of what he is doing, it is at most for practical reasons. He hesitates to act, even after his secret is out, only because he knows that treachery will repel morally conventional minds (D 424 ff.). He has no thought of departing the scene nobly; Schiller even has him pour scorn on people who can 'warm themselves on their will and fine ideas, / Heroes of talk and virtue-bletherers' (D 524 f.). Greater love hath no man for art than this, that he lay down his principles for his central figure to trample on.

Lacking the morally reflective element Schiller's theory requires, all that the main action has left as its tragic point is the Fall of a Great Man, an almost atavistic return to one of the oldest themes of tragedy. Schiller carries it through massively and ceremonially over two whole acts filled with grim ironies and slowly deepening gloom that end in Wallenstein's assassination. But a moral dimension is added by a sub-plot, the tragic love of Max Piccolomini and Wallenstein's daughter Thekla, parted (despite his hero-worship of Wallenstein himself) by Max's loyalty to the Emperor. Without this second and very different focus of interest to provide ethical and poetic relief, Schiller might not have managed to sustain the discipline of sober, unidealized writing overall. But by the same token the love-story comes close to stealing the show. It sets off the brute realities of politics and war and offers the only human warmth and delicacy in Schiller's immense design. And it also shows how much more could blossom from tragic theory than a mere heroics of talk.

Freedom in and freedom from

When Schiller centred his aesthetics on the notion of freedom, not only did it mean he was inevitably made to think about politics; it also led him to ask how far, in what circumstances, and in what sense human beings could ever be free agents—crucial questions for a deviser of drama. The essay *Grace and Dignity* argued that an appearance of freedom in movement, and by extension in human behaviour generally, was possible where the agent was not visibly hemmed in or hindered. Actions could be initiated spontaneously and performed without external pressure or inner conflict. Body and mind, inclination and duty, could be in harmony. Grace was a total 'freedom in' nature. Schiller even identifies a human type—he calls it, somewhat fulsomely, the 'beautiful soul' or 'finer mind' (*schöne Seele*)—which enjoys this ideal integration as its birthright (v. 468).

But the 'freedom in' nature can only be provisional, because in practice life is mostly not like that. Even for those privileged ideal souls, and more obviously for the rest of us, all kinds of pressures wait in the wings to break up the harmony between our sensuous and moral natures. All that the agent can do then is fall back on 'dignity', a defensive inner freedom, a citadel of last retreat. He has lost the initiative to act and can now only react—resist temptation, bear suffering bravely and overcome it mentally, assign a positive sense to brute facts. This is to accept the mind–body split and give an emergency authority to mind. It is an attempt at 'freedom from' nature when acting freely *within* nature has become impossible. Surprisingly, it actually implies a kind of superiority: 'The irresistible power of nature compels us as sensuous beings to recognize our powerlessness, but it reveals in us at the same time a capacity to judge ourselves independent of nature and a superiority over nature on which a quite different kind of self-preservation rests from the one which external nature attacks and imperils' (v. 493).

That is not Schiller's formulation but Kant's; Schiller quotes it however in one of his essays on the Sublime. He might disagree in *Grace and Dignity* with Kant's view that duty was always and necessarily in conflict with inclination, and that this was indeed the very definition of morality; he might conceive instead of an ideal 'inclination *to* duty' which replaced Kant's notion of repeatedly having to overcome an enemy by the ideal of a final reconciliation with him (v. 464 f.). That was to keep an ethical norm in view, just as there is a norm of positive health beyond the necessary remedies for a sick body. But in the circumstances of tragedy Schiller could see there was no such alternative, and a rigorism akin to Kant's necessarily came into its own. It may seem to offer only cold comfort and to be more like stoical teeth-gritting than real freedom. Yet its paradoxical optimism-in-pessimism does rescue something in the face of the ultimate human problem where the only alternative would be simple despair. For an age prepared to believe in a secular spirituality, this was more than a mere stop-gap; and even outside its own historical context it may appeal to the sense that there can indeed be a 'different kind of self-preservation', some way of sustaining personal integrity even in defeat.

The 'Sublime' was a powerful notion in the eighteenth century. The young Schiller had called his heroic criminal Karl Moor 'sublime' (i. 624), and the ambitious Fiesco claimed the term for himself (i. 698): in an obscure way, crime like his could be more exciting and inspiring than virtue, provided it was grandiose enough, not petty. The audience was meant to (and did) respond to Moor's larger-than-lifesize passions, it secretly enjoyed the dreadful consequences, feeling the thrill of 'delightful horror' which Edmund Burke's classic early analysis seized on as the essence of the Sublime. Sublime phenomena—stormy seas, towering peaks, ghostly ruins, immense expanses, dark eerie places—affected the observer so strongly because they all caused something 'analogous to terror . . . the strongest emotion which the mind is capable of feeling': that is, they stirred our instinct of self-preservation. But that hardly explained the seeming perversity of *enjoying* such effects, nor the fashion in taste that went with it (this was the age of the Gothic novel). Perhaps a deprived age in which reasonableness had reigned, and 'the Beautiful' had been reduced to a trivial rococo prettiness, simply needed more exciting stimulants for its imagination.

At all events, Schiller's early plays were close to Gothic effect with their awesome crimes, wild gestures, and *en passant* slaughter of beautiful women—Karl Moor's sweetheart, Fiesco's wife. Yet equally they had an element of potential moral grandeur: Moor purging his oath to the robbers by murder and giving himself up to the law, Fiesco torn between ruthless ambition and a democratic impulse to renounce power. Those were sublime effects too. The trouble was that the moral grandeur in these cases was hard to separate from the indiscriminate onslaught on the spectator in which the young dramatist plainly revelled.

By the mid-1790s, that obvious early fascination of Schiller's with moral conflict had been strengthened, while the urge to dramatize it at all costs and by whatever means had moderated. This personal development matched—and was in part shaped by—a philosophical development culminating in Kant which had, precisely, separated out a rational, moral essence from the crude Gothic effects of the Sublime, and now offered a respectable explanation for its charms. Embarrassed no doubt by the sowing of aesthetic wild oats with which the phenomenon of the Sublime presented them, the thinkers in question traced its paradoxical pleasures not to the emotion of 'terror' itself which Burke had described, but to the observer's instantaneous reaction: faced with something too immense to grasp or too overwhelming to resist, we are forced back—as contrast, refuge, reassurance—upon the rational and moral powers that give humanity its special status. Something of that dramatic sequence is captured in one of Kant's most famous sayings, the statement at the end of the *Critique of Practical Reason* that 'two things fill the mind with ever new and growing admiration and awe, the more often and persistently we reflect upon them: the starry heavens above me and the moral law within me.'

This rationalizing and moralizing of the Sublime was a shift in the balance of power—power of two radically disparate kinds. It also entailed a semantic shift, in that the terrifying objects which were formerly thought of as themselves sublime (which by its etymology means 'elevated') were now merely a means to elevate the observer, or in tragedy the sufferer and the sympathizing audience. What was now truly elevated was the operation of the human mind and spirit in response to suffering.

Schiller glimpses this point (v. 550) but nevertheless goes on using the term 'sublime' for the whole tragic sequence from outside pressure to rational response, with its peculiar bitter-sweet effect. It is as well he does, because it helps to prevent morality as such from taking over as the real point of tragic art. He was fully aware that this usurpation would not do, would indeed be historically regressive: it was only in his lifetime that art had begun to break free from the moralistic demands of religious and other orthodoxies and to claim laws and liberties of its own. That was a clear development from the Enlightenment's campaign for freedom of thought, and it had the same enemies. As late as 1788, Schiller's poem 'The Gods of Greece' had been the target of Christian attacks. Later, as he worked out the moral rights and wrongs of a *Wallenstein* scene, it was brought home to him 'how empty the moral element by itself is' (to Goethe, 27 Feb. 1798). Any rigid doctrine, any foregone conclusion, must be the death of true art. Only morality as process could make living art. Which meant realizing for the stage characters of flesh and blood for whom, 'idealists' though they might be in Schiller's technical sense, morality would not be a pat answer but a struggle all the way. Any victory over nature must not be the easy doing of supermen whom suffering could not touch nor happiness tempt, but the hard result of living and thinking a dilemma through to a necessary sticking-point, a moment of truth where they discovered their own deepest nature. Max Piccolomini, though often quoted—glibly—as an exponent of glib moralism, is a good example of the opposite; he is credible and human because of what it visibly costs him to abandon Wallenstein for the Emperor and thereby to cut himself off from Thekla. It is one of the play's finest touches that he actually needs and appeals for her help (D 2061 ff.) in taking that decision—the very opposite of the effect Wallenstein's supporters tried to ensure by bringing the young couple together in the first place: 'If he really loves you, his decision / Will soon be taken', they say. She agrees, but in her own sense: 'His decision / Will soon be taken, never fear. Decision! / What is there to decide?' (D 1359 f.). She knows him better than he knows himself—somehow he has lived through fifteen years of war without an experience of moral dilemma. Helping him to bring about their final separation is an act of love for the person he really is and now has consciously to become.

So the reflection which crisis sets going in the tragic protagonist is not so much an open debate as an uncovering of personal necessity. Outer necessity gives rise to an inner one: that, paradoxically, is what moral 'freedom' means. Crisis pares the character down to his real identity.

Or *her* identity. For Schiller's next two tragic figures are women. Both are implicated, passively or actively, in the processes of history, which remains the necessary arena in which to show what human beings can be faced with and what they are capable of. *Mary Stuart* (*Maria Stuart*, 1801) draws the starkest possible contrast of history and morality. The Queen of Scots is near the end of her life, a prisoner about to be the victim of rigged political justice. But she is just as much a victim of the political and sexual passions of the Catholics who are trying to free her, and a prisoner ultimately of the world of politics itself in which she has always moved. So it is not gratuitous heroics when she finally embraces the death-sentence passed on her publicly for one thing as a means to atone privately for another. She has not been party to the most recent plot against Elizabeth, but she was guilty years before of Darnley's murder. It now weighs on her, for itself and as a symbol of the intrigues, sexual and political and often both intertwined, which have been her life, and which seem to be the inescapable nature of history.

Aptly or ironically, what seals her fate and makes her atonement possible is the continuing operation of that same mixture. Mary's execution is finally decided not by the imperatives of Protestant politics (though we see the debates in the council-chamber) but by the envy and resentment of an emotionally starved Elizabeth, who in order to be queen has given up everything social and sensual that Mary the woman enjoyed. What is in part—the part that best fits Schiller's theory—the tragedy of Mary's self-purification, and might also have been an austere tragedy of *raison d'état* (dynastic politics demands judicial murder, and hence Elizabeth's moral self-sacrifice for the good of her nation), thus becomes a psycho-drama purporting to lay bare what really makes the powerful in history tick. Namely, nothing more elevated than makes the rest of us tick. As an account of history this is not necessarily wrong or implausible; no doubt personal pique and basic instincts do enter into political decisions. That is merely one possible answer to the question which all historical drama asks, whether great events are played out in a realm and by people different in kind from the everyday? The trouble is that the elements which stress sexual and personal motivation, every one a vital prop to the plot, are all Schiller's invention, from the lurid figure of a Catholic fanatic obsessed with Mary's attractions, via the quixotic passion that makes Leicester intrigue to free her instead of maximizing his career chances at court, down to the violent meeting of the two queens which destroys Mary's last hope of being freed. Mary's triumph in this slanging-match—in substance it is as crude as that—makes her death certain. It is not so much the demands of *Realpolitik* (though we see plenty of that) as the memory of this humiliation by a more than merely dynastic rival, and in front of her favourite, that makes a wavering Elizabeth finally sign the death-warrant. This is the world from which Mary's atonement and death rescue her; her self-purification is an escape from history itself. Elizabeth is left embroiled in history, safe now on her throne and politically in control, but emotionally defeated and alone. Leicester has hastily left the country.

Mary Stuart has been much admired as a product of Schiller's 'High Classicism', for its formal control (it contains some of his serenest pentameters) and for its elegant structural symmetry (it focuses alternately on Mary and Elizabeth, has two acts of hope and uncertainty preparing two of tragic resignation, with the decisive meeting in a pivotal Act Three). Yet the sensationalizing of political motive means it is already halfway to being a 'witches' cauldron of raging romance'. That was George Bernard Shaw's description of Schiller's next play, *The Maid of Orleans* (*Die Jungfrau von Orleans*, 1802). Schiller himself called it 'a Romantic tragedy', for obvious reasons: the Classicist here lets himself go, plunging into the medieval miracles and mysteries of the Joan of Arc story and adding highly coloured effects and inexplicable events of his own, like warnings from a ghostly knight and thunderclaps which convey the divine judgement. But Schiller also keeps the pattern of sin and atonement familiar from *Mary Stuart*, right down to the motif of accepting a right judgement for the wrong sin. Joan is untrue to

91

her mission in mid-battle, falling on sight for an Englishman she should have been killing on sight. Her guilt keeps her silent when she is accused of devilry; she has to suffer rejection and humiliation before she can regain divine favour. But the 'moral' element is now a less plausible focus of attention. Joan's lapse is a gratuitous importation into the legend, where Mary's transgression was a convincing part of her personal past. Just as gratuitously, Schiller then changes the historical ending which is virtually the legend's emblem, Joan's death at the stake. Her martyrdom would have fitted his theory well enough; but he had already presented one passive female death, and whatever else he was doing, he was consciously seeking dramatic variety. So he has the captive Joan regain her powers through penance, break her bonds like Samson, and die a heroic death on the battlefield (though there is no obvious dramatic reason why a Joan unburned, escaped, and her atonement completed, need die at all).

The divergence from history has often been enough to discredit the play. Yet clearly Schiller was trying to do something other than show again 'how it really was' in any immediate historical sense. Through the steam rising from the cauldron, we can make out a version of his familiar myth of primal innocence. In Joan's story, for once in history, innocence triumphs on a grand scale; the simple country girl shames the lax, defeatist court and changes the course of the war. But her story contains the bitter lesson—which is no doubt why Schiller kept its basic shape—that wonders *do* cease; the religious-cum-military idyll is doomed to remain an episode. The pull of his tragic theory led him to explain the unhappy ending by a moral flaw in the heroine, where Shaw's *Saint Joan*, by contrast, analyses external factors—the mystery and volatility of army morale, the dependence of Joan's success on Dunois's good generalship and logistical organization in the background, the role of changed fighting methods and of the shift from feudal to national allegiance, and above all the uneasy relation between the ardent convictions of a future saint and the limitations and resentments of the men whose cause she is serving. The end of her 'little hour of miracles' is inherent in a complex historical situation.

Yet in making Joan's flaw the at first sight merely romantic one of sexual attraction, Schiller was moving towards the substantial theme of sexual politics, not now as that phrase applies to *Mary Stuart*, but in a more modern sense. Everyone around Joan—crassly, considering the task she has taken on—urges her to be a 'normal' woman. The French generals compete for her love, the court presses her to accept one of them, her superstitious father regards her from the outset as a 'grave aberration of nature'. Reversing the roles in Shakespeare's *1 Henry VI*, it is the father who disowns the daughter; it is his accusation of devilry that she cannot answer, the weight of his authority is as important as her other 'guilt'. The ghostly knight's warning that she must push her mission no further sets another, unexplained, limit on her activity. She also has secret yearnings that undermine her mission: though pastoral innocence was the source of her strength, for the girl within the warrior it is also a lost paradise she yearns to go back to. Everything conspires to drive Joan out of her historic role, just as everything conspired to trap Mary in hers. It is not irrelevant that the two heroines are complementary figures in the intricate sub-categories of Schiller's tragic theory, the one embodying 'sublimity of composure', the other 'sublimity of action'. That could be translated into modern terms if we see Mary as the woman rebelling against her role as a sexual object, passive even in politics, and Joan as the woman struggling to play an active role free from sexual connotation.

At times Schiller tired of writing historical drama, of the desperate struggle with yet another set of sources, the long slog before they began to come alive imaginatively and take shape as drama. Yet he always returned to history in the end; it was the ballast his creativity needed. Clearly, even history was far from crushing his inventive imagination, which reshaped it freely. But there was something far more arbitrary about constructing purely fictive situations where the only limit to human suffering was how much malice the imagination could impute to fate. This was made plain after *The Maid of Orleans*, when Schiller took the one break from history of his mature years and once more invented a plot for the first time since his beginnings. In fact *The Bride of Messina* (*Die Braut von Messina*, 1803) goes right back to the theme of two feuding brothers from *The Robbers*. Once again they love the same woman. But this time, for rather more than good measure, she is also their sister, secretly sent away at birth to foil (as it turns out, of course, to fulfil) the prophecy that she would cause both her brothers' death. It all very obviously echoes *Oedipus*, and the Greek effect is what Schiller was after. He emphasizes it by the range of his metrical forms, and especially by using a Greek-style chorus such as he had been experimenting with in sketches for a drama on the Knights of Malta (iii. 160 f.). The dramatic point however is not Greek. Destiny in *The Bride* creates a denouement where clear-sighted choice can replace blind involvement and end the tragic sequence. It looks as if Schiller has gone to extremes, piling disastrous secrecy and chance on top of a family curse and an irrational fate to construct a catastrophe that will fully test— and vindicate—the moral powers his theory rests on. 'Only a free death breaks the chain of destiny': the survivor speaks this quotable line (2641) at the funeral of the brother he has killed, as a preface to immediate suicide. Or so it would have been, if an obscure sense of proprieties had not led Schiller to separate the two ceremonies (to Goethe, 26 Jan. 1803). This creates a literal and figurative breathing-space in which an issue that might have seemed morally clear-cut becomes humanly complicated. Instead of the prompt heroic gesture of self-immolation, there is a drawn-out ending full of confused and anything but moral impulses. The survivor still incestuously loves his sister, envies the devotion which he feels his dead brother will now enjoy, desperately seeks and gets reassurance that he too is loved, before finally—dying. Once again the theoretical model for tragedy shows through, but its rational lines are blurred by darker emotions. As so often with Schiller, the play can only be read schematically if we disregard the human detail. And the human detail composes the play we experience.

As important as Schiller's Greek experiment itself was the chance it gave him to make his position clear on a larger issue. When he saw the play performed, he felt that for the first time he had achieved 'a real tragedy' (to Körner, 28 Mar. 1803). On the other hand most of the audience were alienated by the 'unnatural' chorus. If Schiller was perhaps fixated on the Greek ideal, were they not more narrowly and damagingly fixated on a crude idea of the 'natural' and its place in art? The essay *On Naïve and Reflective Poetry* had operated with a distinction between '*mere* nature' and the 'true' or 'real' nature which poets should try to represent; but very probably Schiller's audience had not read that work, and were unthinkingly happy with the contemporary novels and plays that transposed everyday life directly into 'art', direct descendants of the inert version of bourgeois drama that ousted the young Schiller's social radicalism from the Mannheim stage. In their youth Goethe and Schiller had indeed done a lot to bring art closer to life—psychologically, formally, socially, nationally. For that very reason they were now aghast at these banal excrescences from the revolutionary roots they had set.

By the time Schiller published *The Bride of Messina*, he had come to see his use of the chorus as a means of 'declaring war openly and honestly on naturalism in art', as 'a living wall which tragedy draws around it to close itself off from the real world' (ii. 819). This was not just a sudden perverse shift to the opposite extreme in reaction against crude naturalism, and certainly not a movement towards art for art's sake. Rather it was 'the last, the decisive step' (an earlier one had been the use of dramatic verse) in a process of clarifying through practice what exactly art is. Namely *not* illusionism. In art, none of the externals—stage lighting, or stage sets, or metrical language, to take the specifics of drama—is 'real'. They only *represent* real things, they are conventional not natural signs. So surely the onstage action itself cannot be an exception, it is not (so to speak) a real bull in a semiotic china-shop. Schiller remembers the seventeenth-century champions of the unities who treated stage time and place as if they were real time and place and condemned all plots to be played out in a single location and a single day. It is a nice polemical paradox that he can lump together those discredited extremes of an old Classicism with the writers and consumers of a new naturalism.

His own positive view is an even greater paradox: that every detail of a work of art must be 'ideal' if the whole is truly to represent reality (ii. 818). The concept 'ideal' has nothing to do with elevation or ennoblement, it means here 'permeated by the action of the mind'—Schiller has already said that art helps us to 'shift the sensuous world . . . to an objective distance, turn it into a free work of our minds, and control materiality through ideas' (ii. 816 f.). It is in that sense that art cannot be content with 'the appearance of truth' (which, paradoxically again, is what you get by plumping down bits of reality untransformed on the stage) but rather 'builds its ideal edifice on the deep and firm foundation of nature' (ii. 817). Naturalism is no way to nature. But realism is, and true realism is attained when world and mind interpenetrate in an achieved style. And style, as Goethe wrote in the same spirit, 'rests on the deepest foundations of knowledge, on the nature of things in so far as we are permitted to perceive it in visible and graspable forms'. In other words, art is a crowning of cognition.

The Classical aesthetic was thus no sort of turn away from reality, as has sometimes been suggested. Witness Schiller's last completed play, which goes back to politics, to the political theme of crucial importance for his age and obsessively present in nearly all his work: legitimacy and rebellion, and the legitimacy *of* rebellion.

On the surface Schiller could not have had a more random occasion for writing *William Tell* (*Wilhelm Tell*, 1804); he did so in response to a persistent Weimar rumour that he already was. Yet the subject was as if made for much that he still had to say—about mankind and nature, freedom and tyranny, morality and revolution, individualism and the collective, present action and awareness of the past. Nature in *William Tell* both grounds and dwarfs human actions. Though Austrian oppression is powerfully evoked, the natural setting of Switzerland—which Schiller realizes in lyrical and descriptive passages that go beyond the normal scope of drama—seems from the first to promise freedom. The lake storms that twice help fugitives to escape are an almost allegorical ally. And when the Swiss are made to build a fortress to serve their own oppression, it is symbolically overshadowed by the mountains all around (373 ff.). That is omen enough before Tell ever speaks the words 'what hands have built, hands can overthrow.' In the same way, the proposition 'beneath the tyrants' feet the ground is hollow' (2408) is already true in essence before the conspiracy against them has begun—true in proportion as the Swiss, by contrast, feel their native ground firm and a source of strength under their own feet. This is, among other things, a play about territoriality, about the intimate link between roots and rights, about the rebirth of national solidarity under alien pressure. Resistance takes shape before our eyes, despite visible friction between Swiss communities and social classes. Just over the threshold into the nineteenth century, the century of the nation state, *William Tell* is the first drama of Romantic nationalism.

But it is also a drama of Classical restraint. It is not just foreign tyranny that the sublime setting puts into perspective. The night-time meeting at the Rütli where the cantons renew their ancient alliance ends with a symbolic sunrise touching the peaks above them (1438 ff.). The conspirators stand humbly looking up, not (as in so much revolutionary art, including Swiss portrayals of Tell like Ferdinand Hodler's) monumentalized, but kept to a human scale by the same surroundings that give them their conviction of natural right. So close to nature at its most grandiose, it makes immediate sense to see a revolt against tyranny as restoring the 'ancient primal state of nature, where man stands face to face with man'—sword in hand, if need be (1281 ff.). Not however in a posture of heroism, much less a state of intoxication with political intrigue for its own sake, but simply of determination to defend the natural things of life—land, wife, children—against attack. If that is natural and necessary, it is a self-limiting necessity: violent action has to end as soon as the attack has been warded off. There is no natural justification for vengefulness.

No group of conspirators was ever more anxious for moderation and legality than Schiller's Swiss. 'What must be, let it be; but go no further. / Let us chase out these governors and their henchmen / Over our borders, batter down their castles, / But, if it can be, without blood'. For healthy respect is earned by 'a people / That, sword in hand, still acts with moderation' (1365 ff.). Schiller's dramatic presentation itself follows the same principle; even the minimum of collective violence needed to drive out the Austrians is not shown on stage. 'The destruction of a Bastille carried out by one man, with German calm and a little hammer', was Benjamin Constant's comment.

The one visible violent act is Tell's, and that is ruthless and effective. He waits in ambush and kills in cold blood. After the horror of having to shoot the apple from his son's head, the next bolt necessarily had to be for Governor Gessler, not in mere revenge but to prevent further atrocity. It is an act, not of passionate vendetta but of phlegmatic resolution—here and elsewhere, Schiller captures the temperament as remarkably as he does the scenery of a nation he had never visited (cf. to Cotta, 27 June 1804). Strikingly, unlike the Tell of old Swiss chronicle, Schiller's Tell has never been part of the conspiracy. He seems politically inert, even quietistic (420), he declares himself not a man for political councils, though offering to act when needed (442 ff.). The pattern is familiar from *Fiesco*—there too democrats were upstaged by an individualist. Here their achievement of solidarity is lovingly celebrated, but they do not perform the decisive act. This time, of course, there is not the haze of moral uncertainty which surrounded the loner and his motives in *The Conspiracy of Fiesco*. Tell has none of Fiesco's private ambition for public power and glory; instead, he links the private world and its values with the public sphere by striking back when struck at. This makes him a representative figure in his way, representative of all the individual interests which the Rütli conspiracy consciously subsumes, but which he insists on safeguarding with his own hands. (In a coda to his dramatic action, Schiller has him spell out—somewhat self-righteously—his justification for murdering Gessler.)

Schiller's play thus operates somewhat awkwardly with two stages of political generalization. If the conspirators are perhaps closer to his ideal, as the solemn poetic tone of those scenes suggests, they cannot compete for dramatic effect with Tell's legendary figure and actions. Yet the differences between Tell and the Rütli conspirators matter less than their common achievement, which is the humane conduct of a revolution. When Schiller bowed to popular rumour and took on the subject, he discovered in Swiss history the liberal's last chance. Here was an overthrow of unjust power that did not produce a different kind of unjust power; a nation of coolheads refuted pessimistic expectations of what must happen when the bonds of civil order, however justifiably, are loosened. The verse inscription in a copy of the play Schiller gave Dalberg made this explicit. One stanza evokes the case where a chaos of primitive forces overwhelms justice and casts the state adrift, a second the very different case of pious, pastoral folk who cast off oppression but temper anger with humanity and triumph with modesty. Against the disillusioning example of France in his lifetime is set a crumb of optimism, or at least a plausible counter-example, even if finding it meant going all the way back to the medieval past. No subsequent revolution, of course, was to live up to the ethical standards of *William Tell* (at least until the 1989 revolutions in Eastern Europe, which are at present unfinished business). Still, it is apt that after years of wrestling with the ethics as well as the aesthetics of political action, Schiller's theatre should end in this historical idyll, this Utopian overthrow, with its passionate moderation and its implied renewal of hope in history.

Or not *quite* end. Only drama itself has such neat conclusions, and Schiller was soon deep in new materials and a new theme: sixteenth-century Russia under Boris Godunov, Dmitri's bid for the throne, and the subtle dilemma of the convinced claimant who discovers, just as he wins power, that he is not after all the true heir. A dilemma so subtle that to Thomas Mann it seemed to be less a matter of politics and history than, deep down, an allegory of self-doubt from a writer who had to struggle against the odds all his life in order to prove his value and establish his status. Maybe it is indeed just such cross-threads of inner experience that at the deepest level give a dramatist the power of empathy, and make his creations live. But in every observable sense Schiller had won that struggle. He had known self-doubt in plenty. But he had come to a clear psychological and historical understanding of his own talent, and within the limits of its malleability had shaped it to his conscious purposes. He had mastered his theatrical craft and seen it honoured. He had learned to accept, and been befriended and partnered by, the outstanding poet of his time and place. He had also, after years of overwork, just about achieved financial security for himself and his family. At forty-six, he might now have looked forward to working his way steadily down his list of projects. History still beckoned.

Conclusion: real and ideal

Lifetime

Schiller's forty-six years were divided evenly between the narrow, enforced passivity of his education and the narrow, intense activity of his working career. There is little other content to his adult life but thinking and writing: no outward excitement after the legendary episode of his escape from Württemberg, no significant travel after the wanderings of his early exile, hardly any social contacts apart from his intellectual communings with Körner, Goethe, Humboldt. He did marry and have children. Otherwise the substance of his life was the desk, the pen, the reflective and creative mind. In the fullest, most consuming existential sense, Schiller *was* a writer. He lived out the kind of specialization which, on his own theory of culture, was vital to human progress but ruinous to the individual human being.

True, creative writing had a special place in that theory and he could declare, when he returned to poetry after years of philosophizing, that the philosopher was a caricature and the poet the only true human being (to Goethe, 7 Jan. 1795). Abstraction, that is, though a necessary tool for analysing the ills of modern culture, was itself one of them, whereas poetry uniquely exemplified and restored wholeness. Yet in practice, as a professional writer who had to work hard for his living, the poet too was abstracted from the fullness of life, however rich his imaginative experience might be. And on this Schiller was acutely aware that his was frustratingly meagre beside Goethe's. 'You have a kingdom to rule over', he wrote, 'where I only have a somewhat numerous family of concepts' (to Goethe, 31 Aug. 1794). Part of the problem lay with what their respective imaginations had to draw on. Life itself set limits. Schiller's image of 'a kingdom' was almost literally true of his friend. With his elevated position and easy circumstances, Goethe was able to travel freely, he helped administer the

Duchy of Weimar, he moved in society there and in other German-speaking lands, he met many of the great and powerful of Europe. He even went as a privileged observer on a military campaign, when the German princes invaded revolutionary France in 1792. It was all grist to the literary mill; Goethe's broad experience and robust vitality nourished a massive *œuvre*. Schiller lacked both. His existence was shaped accordingly. When ill (which was frequently), he kept to his room; when well, he kept to his room and wrote. Whatever ideal functions poetry might have, in practice it did nothing for his health. On the contrary. Poetry, he wrote ruefully, was an activity of the whole man and consequently demanded the strength of the whole man: 'the Muses drain you dry' (to Goethe, 29 Aug. 1795). It was the experience of art that made people whole, not its creation; it almost seems as if the artist has to make a correspondingly total sacrifice.

It would have been hard to live that wearing and monopolizing desk life without a conviction that the 'ideal' operations of the mind made some difference to the 'real' world beyond the desk. Schiller had that root conviction, inherited from the Enlightenment, in its fiercest form. He was not primarily, as Goethe was, a self-expressive writer, creating literature from a distinctive personal experience and an infinitely varied response to the world. In that respect at least, whatever the arguments of the essay *On Naïve and Reflective Poetry*, he was the less modern writer of the two. He stood in the older tradition of a pragmatic aesthetic, seeking to persuade, impress, move, and inspire, embodying and appealing to that 'family of concepts' of his which were also in part public property, the shared experience and achievement of his age. His early plays had arraigned a society in the name of freedom and justice, and at the same time made plain the pitfalls of pursuing these ideals. His mature essays diagnose and prescribe for the ills of contemporary politics and modern culture in the name of a social and ultimately an existential harmony. His later plays offer object lessons in how to live with the harshness of history and still stay human. They also build up a cumulative critique of politics and *raison d'état* as correspondingly inhuman. Of his poetry, the ballads much favoured by nineteenth-century readers tell stories that validate some ethically uplifting message by a happy ending; but there are also, to balance them, a number of philosophical poems (relatively neglected then and now) which look into the abyss beneath hope and aspiration, and brace the reader to realize that humanity has to set its own values and impart its own fleeting warmth to existence. Other poems again, grandiose historical or anthropological constructs, run a synoptic eye over great sweeps of time and set all individual human effort in a sobering perspective. Everything Schiller wrote is ultimately a pointer to, constructs a clear framework for, human—and humane—practice.

Finally, more down to earth and of his time, there is Schiller's work as a literary activist, his tireless organizing and initiating—formally, as the editor of a succession of journals and poetry yearbooks for which he diplomatically and single-mindedly gathered other writers in the good cause of raising literary standards; but also informally, by stimulating other minds through personal contact, what Humboldt called 'the silent and almost magical effect of great spiritual natures' on their contemporaries, of which the printed word passed down to posterity is only the 'mummified' form. Here Schiller's great *coup*—far too great to have been planned, nor could he even have guessed it was necessary—was to give a new impulse to Goethe's work just when the literary landscape around the older poet seemed discouragingly bleak. Schiller became Goethe's prime audience and interlocutor, an enthusiastic reader yet also a perceptive critic of works still in the making. He welcomed with open arms, and a sure eye for what separates literature from pornography, the erotic poems which even the Duke of Weimar advised Goethe not to publish. It was partly his curiosity that sent Goethe back to the unfinished *Faust*, and his lucidity that helped to clarify its deepest themes. 'You have given me a second poetic youth,' Goethe wrote gratefully at the time (6 Jan. 1798); and many years later, 'I really do not know what would have become of me without Schiller's stimulus' (to C. L. F. Schultz, 10 Jan. 1829).

Schiller's stimulus was the soul of a partnership that transformed the literary landscape and established a German Classicism. The term 'Classicism' suggests something settled and accepted, but that is an illusion of historical distance. Creating this Classicism was a matter not just of tranquil poetic composition, but of hard struggle. To begin with, there was a German public that needed educating—a didactic poet of our century, Bertolt Brecht, neatly picking up the leitmotif that runs through Schiller's work and character, calls the two men's joint efforts 'a high-minded conspiracy against the public'. Schiller himself, when most provoked by the public's inertia, saw the only right relation to it as 'war' (to Goethe, 25 June 1799). That may seem a strange choice of route towards an ideal of harmony; but then, like all the great cultural critics, Schiller was concerned to give society what it needed, not what it wanted (and no cultural critic ever thought through those needs so thoroughly). 'Harmony' would be on his terms.

The same combativeness was Schiller's response to the older generation of writers he and Goethe found themselves confronted and, they often felt, baulked by—a residual fading Enlightenment with no understanding for a modern poetry that went beyond rationalism to embrace the full 'empirical pathological condition of man' (Goethe to Schiller, 25 Nov. 1797). And there was also—more insidious yet, since at least those older rivals would in time fade out completely—a younger Romantic generation, already turning away from the Classical ideal of 'living shape' to a religiose medievalism and a fantastical spirituality. A foot-dragging past, then, and a future intent on relapsing: they were equally enemies of a Classical aesthetic which (however insoluble the mind–body problem might be in philosophy or medicine) had found a way in literature to balance the claims of spirit and matter. It was war on two fronts, and for Schiller a holy war. Revealingly, he calls his new journal, *Horae* (*Die Horen*), launched in the mid-nineties, a 'Church Militant' (to Goethe, 1 Nov. 1795). The phrase hits off his combination of doctrinal commitment and belligerence, something there was ample scope for when the new works and ideas published in that journal met with resistance, and the right reaction seemed to be outright satire and polemic. Goethe is wholeheartedly with him, but Schiller plays the roles of ideologue and strategist in the campaign through which they established their authority.

The clarity, energy, single-mindedness, even sometimes

ruthlessness, which the cultural moment called for were not just literary qualities but signs of a larger potential. So that Goethe's comment years later on the table-talk—'Schiller appears here, as always, in absolute possession of his sublime nature; he is as great at the tea-table as he would have been in the Council of State'—contains in a nutshell the history of eighteenth-century energies that went into literature because there was no way they could flow straight into society. They had to shape the dialectic of mind and body in works of art and theoretical essays because they could not take part directly in that larger practical experiment in mind–body relations, history.

And yet Schiller's work intertwines with history as closely as that exclusion clause will allow. His dramatic activity is first set going by the pressures of absolutism; the highpoint of his philosophical work is a response to absolutism's final crisis; his greatest drama, *Wallenstein*, looks back to the turmoil that created modern European absolutism from amid the turmoil of events that is shaping its successor; and the dramas of his last phase feel for a firm moral footing in that new turmoil of Napoleonic war and political change. Whatever the fictional settings, it is all very close to the realities of his time. The insistent return of the word 'Ideal' in Schiller's writings has always made it easy to caricature him as an ethereal dreamer staring up in vain at a vacant sky. Yet in context the word is never vacuous but always dense with desired reality, of a very earthly kind; and the ideals with which Schiller responded to the reigning reality of his day return insistently in later times because they are real human needs. The publicity vital to society as an open forum, for which the younger Enlightenment Schiller argued, is in Russian 'glasnost'; its devotees elsewhere in Eastern Europe unite in an embryonic 'New' or 'Civic' Forum; the pressure for change in repressive societies builds up in response not just to the fact of repression but to the way it imposes a reduced and unbalanced humanity, which (Schiller showed) destroys equally the means and the ends of politics; and the pressure may then wring change from rigidly closed societies through the revolt which was at the centre of so much of his work—with luck, through non-violent revolution such as he celebrated in his last finished play. The Idealist, it seems, is as close to earth as the Realist; he merely does not accept the limiting Reality Principle, but holds to his own Possibility Principle—even when its demands seem to verge on the impossible. As Schiller wrote in his last letter to Wilhelm von Humboldt: 'after all, we are both idealists, and we would be ashamed if people were to say that things shaped us and not we them' (2 April 1805).

Legacy

Not much German practice, historically, has matched the best of German thought and feeling. It is true that Schiller's and Goethe's 'high-minded conspiracy' was eventually successful to the extent that the public came to accept them and their works as the classics of the national literature. But, as in any culture, this was no guarantee that the substance of their work—its humane ideals, its ethical discriminations—would be absorbed. To begin with, Goethe's and Schiller's achievement answered above all the cruder needs of German self-esteem after centuries in which Germany had lagged behind the other cultures of Europe, France especially. Now there was a German national literature, and a belated Classicism too, recognized even in France through the agency of Madame de Staël and prized, written about, and translated by the English Romantics and Victorians.

German pride focused the more intensely on culture because Germany was still not a political nation; if culture was one important possession of real nations, to have a prestigious one was almost a promise of nationhood. But there is something wrong with the idea of 'possessing' culture. It shuts up the energies of art and thought in a showcase. It spawns what Nietzsche called the 'culture-philistine', by which he meant not the person who lacks and spurns culture but the person who appropriates and makes much of culture yet remains inwardly untouched by it. (For example, in 1871 there were even claims that victory in the Franco-Prussian War meant German culture had defeated French culture.)

The result is in every sense a monumental misunderstanding. In 1859, with German aspirations for national unity rising to a peak, celebrations for the hundredth anniversary of Schiller's birth turned into a political demonstration on a scale unprecedented in Germany. Orators full of national enthusiasm lifted the speeches on unity from *William Tell* as if medieval Switzerland and nineteenth-century Germany were identical cases. They played down or ignored the Classical ideal of cosmopolitan humanity and harped on Schiller's German-ness, though his work shows little sign of a specifically national commitment—there is perhaps only the early appeal (which he did not try to fulfil himself) for a theatre of German subjects (v. 830) and the poem-fragment 'German Greatness' of 1797 where he contrasts the essential other-worldliness of Germany with the great warring acquisitive powers, France and Britain, who were then currently carving up the real world between them (i.472 ff.). For nationalists in 1859, Schiller was simply a convenient emblem—noble in stance, rhetorically quotable in style—on which to focus mass enthusiasm. But when masses acclaim (or revile) a writer, it is always doubtful how many have read him and how well. The centenary misuse of Schiller's authority, though still relatively mild, was a first step towards the propaganda of the Nazi era, 'Schiller as a comrade in arms of Hitler' (an actual book title of 1932). Culture and its prestige are always at risk from political piracy.

Less obvious, but insidious at a deep level, was another scenario of cultural prejudice in which Schiller had a central role, this time through appearing in an unfavourable light. The fine discriminations and conciliatory balance of his essay *On Naïve and Reflective Poetry* were too delicate to be held steady by simpler minds; it was easier to turn the whole matter into a distinction between on the one hand spontaneous 'real' poetry and on the other an all too deliberate surrogate, discredited from the start because it needed the reflective mind to make up for deficient genius. The ground had been prepared for this irrationalist prejudice, all unwittingly, by the dramatist Lessing when he disclaimed for himself the title of 'true poet' (the German *Dichter*, a word to conjure with) and confessed to the hydraulic contrivances that had replaced the flowing spring of genius he lacked. A great writer's modesty is always gratefully received by the grudging, and this scrupulous self-criticism has been used as a blunt instrument against his reputation ever since. After Schiller's plainly confessional essay, the dichotomy hardened, the more so because some of the young Romantics actively played off the great 'natural' poet Goethe against his less fortunately endowed partner, scorning the notion of 'reflective' poetry as a mere euphemism for poetic feebleness. The partnership itself was represented as an unequal, even a presumptuous pairing. (Nietzsche, in his most assertive and unargued mode, was later to object to the very linkage 'Goethe *and* Schiller.) The crudely dismissive typology that resulted from all this, with its key norm of the indefinable *Dichter*, planted a seed of anti-intellectualism at the heart of Europe's most intellectual culture. The plant flourished dismayingly in the irrationalist climate of the late nineteenth century. By the early twentieth century, any mere 'writer' (*Schriftsteller* or *Literat*) who also ventured to think—men of the stature of Thomas Mann, Hermann Broch, Robert Musil—was likely to suffer from the shotgun criticism it allowed, while the honorific title *Dichter* went to the exponents of sometimes all too naive intuitions which were blithely held to transcend thought. Pretentious poetasters sometimes claimed the benefit of these facile assumptions. Behind the ostracizing of reflection there lay among other things a reluctance to think critically about social and political realities, an evasion into what claimed to be 'timeless' literature, not in the sense of work that would outlast its time, but of work that would allegedly have been sullied by any contact with it. Such false fastidiousness was inevitably political, by default and through the ideals it entailed—the Great Permanencies of (usually bucolic) Being, set simplistically against the evils of modern life. The line leads down to the irrationalist ideology and 'Blood and Soil' literature of Nazism; to the brief triumph of its cultural fellow-travellers who were happy to see their rivals damned as 'degenerate'; and to the traumatic exile of nearly every German writer who mattered. This and much more was a heavy price to pay for the exorcizing of an old foolishness; but at least now the honorifics and pejoratives have gone. Since 1945 no one sets himself up as a *Dichter* any more. Brecht almost as a public demonstration, chose the sober designation 'play-writer' (*Stückeschreiber*) for himself; modern German writers feel free to reflect unashamedly.

But Schiller's work also left a less debased legacy than this pathological politics of culture. German intellectual history of the nineteenth century and beyond, from aesthetics and psychology to sociology and politics, bears his mark. 'Schiller's felicitous ideas', Goethe wrote as he watched them unfold, 'will gradually gain admittance. People will start by contradicting him, and in a few years they will copy him out without acknowledgement' (to Humboldt, 3 Dec. 1795). Something like that happened. The Romantics often sneered and sniped at Schiller, but the criticism and cultural theory they developed in the years around 1800 began from his analysis of modernity and its discontents. Their solutions, it is true, soon diverged from his: where Schiller aspired to a new quasi-Classical form that would contain the modern sensibility and culture, they increasingly accepted the infinite and formless diversity of both. Schiller's ideal of reintegrative play with a lived experience that had been freed from purposes became for them a *dis*integrative play which the arbitrary imagination could revel in. A cultural problem was raised to a creative principle: irony had arrived in modern literature to stay.

The Romantic dilemma and solution, or dilemma renamed 'solution', were then the starting-point for Hegel's *Aesthetics* in the 1820s—but on intellectual terrain still clearly marked out by Schiller. In systematic terms, to be precise, the Romantics were Hegel's finishing-point. For he presented their disharmony between mind and materials as a terminus beyond which there was no other possible relation of Absolute Spirit to the world of objects on which it depended for its realization. This late in history, Spirit looked back on an odyssey from beginnings in a primitive 'Symbolic' art, where objects were only approximate vessels for its expression (as in the profusion and confusion of Indian art) via a 'Classical' integration of subjectivity and objectivity (the obligatory Greek perfection again) to the point where, at the extremity of 'Romantic' (i.e. European vernacular) art, Spirit splits away from matter once more and moves towards pure philosophical abstraction. In other words, with 'the end of the Romantic art-form', art itself teeters on the edge of extinction.

The elements from Schiller's intellectual world are obvious (not for nothing was the young Hegel deeply impressed by the 'masterpiece' of the *Aesthetic Letters* when they first appeared). But if the mature Hegel is still pulled one way by Schillerian concepts and ideals, by the integration of sense and spirit, by Classical harmony and the Greek paradigm, he is pulled the other way by his observation of the new Romantic times—and by the fact that he belongs to them. For by the thin but decisive margin of a decade, he is of a different age from Schiller. Schiller still hopes art may yet create some analogue of Classical perfection in which to capture modernity whole, and he brings art circling back as a culminating fulfilment long after it has served its purpose as an instrument in mankind's linear evolution. For Hegel, art's evolution is itself strictly linear, and it is now at the end of the line. He looks at his disjointed prosaic age and is realistic, pessimistic, even defeatist about the chances of restoring it to or through poetry. And defeat it certainly was, especially when seen the way Hegel saw it, as historically necessary and irreversible. For what had been new about Schiller's thought—indeed about German eighteenth-century aesthetics generally—was precisely that in opposition to previous philosophical and religious orthodoxies, it assigned value to the sensuous and made sense and spirit interdependent. Now the two elements were allegedly drifting apart again for good. Whether Hegel himself lamented this is not clear. His formulations, it is true, do sometimes have an elegiac beauty. But he was after all a philosopher himself. The impending abstraction was his professional element, and everywhere in his system he gives pride of place to Spirit. Earthly impurities, even beauty, could only delay Its final perfect self-awareness.

And Hegel's, in his heyday, was an influential voice. But then a voice every bit as powerful reversed the priorities once more and restated Schiller's demand for human wholeness. The need was more urgent than ever. The *Aesthetic Letters* had shown how division of labour (in the most general sense—Schiller's examples were the philosopher and astronomer, not workingmen) was necessary to human progress, but harmful to individual human beings and ultimately to their society. Since that diagnosis the Industrial Revolution had accelerated, enforced, and exploited the division of labour, turned people almost literally into the component parts of machines, and robbed them of their full selves in ways more debased and debasing than anything Schiller could have imagined. The concrete forms of debasement were plain for those who had eyes to see. But Marx's account of their larger meaning, and his counter-ideal of a society in which human beings would be given back their whole selves, came from a mind steeped in German Classical thought. Though Marx is usually read as a sequel to Hegel, his much more concrete concept of alienation goes back directly to Schiller. Even where his argument seems purely economic, there are sometimes echoes of Schiller's aesthetic humanism: when gifts between tribes are replaced by barter and exchange value, what is lost is an admiration for objects and their workmanship which is close to the aesthetic. Value can inhere in things; it is a matter of how they are looked at and the spirit in which they were made. Mass production is the death of individual creativity. In some ways, as might be expected, Marx is more realistic than the eighteenth-century aesthetic theorists—at last the idealizing of the Greeks is countered by a reminder that their happy wholeness rested on a system of slave-labour. But not in all: when Marx's *German Ideology* foresees a society that will abolish the division of labour into hunter, fisherman, shepherd, and critic, leaving everyone free 'to hunt in the morning, fish in the afternoon, and in the evening raise animals, and also criticize' (if only the meal) he is a good deal more utopian than Schiller, who recognized that divided labour is with us for good and can only be offset, not undone.

There are other beneficiaries yet. The young Nietzsche owes more to Schiller than he likes to admit: the fundamental human drives evoked in *The Birth of Tragedy*—the creative upthrust of the dionysian and the cool shaping power of the apolline—pose a Schillerian problem of integrating antithetical forces. Nietzsche's ambition is not merely to restore whole human beings but to revive flagging modern creativity, in emulation of the rare balance of power once seen in ancient tragedy. (So the Greeks are back again, but at least no longer as an effortlessly serene race: the argument now is that their grim existential insights generated serene form as a means to psychic survival.)

But as with Schiller, the cultural critic's task is to diagnose
what the age lacks and prescribe ways to overcome the defi-
ciency. As with Schiller again, the theory is as much psychological as aesthetic, with anticipations of Freud in the id-like
darkness of the dionysian. And still in the realm of psychology,
a yet more direct line runs from Schiller to Carl Gustav Jung,
part of whose *Psychological Types* is a substantial commentary
on Schiller's two greatest aesthetic arguments—though, oddly
enough, almost all of it is devoted to the *Aesthetic Letters* rather
than to the essay *On Naïve and Reflective Poetry*, whose
typology of Realist and Idealist so much more obviously anticipates Jung's own typology of extrovert and introvert. (Indeed,
Jung seems unable or unwilling to grasp just how radically typological Schiller's analysis is.)

It is a sign of the wholeness of Schiller's thought itself that
it has nourished such diverse and such fundamental enquiries.
To say that his work is 'central' to human concerns is not the
usual cliché but a sober act of location. Yet the other mark of
his continuing presence—in later aesthetics, politics, or
psychology—is division in another sense: antithesis and antag-
onism become the necessary terms in which problems are
posed. Schiller may not be the only begetter of that German
tradition of thinking in opposites, but he is surely its decisive
exponent, the one who handles it with the most dazzling stylistic virtuosity and the one who confirmed it at a crucial point in
German intellectual history as *the* mode of truly radical analysis. Hegel's thesis and antithesis, Schopenhauer's will and
representation, Heine's Hellene and Nazarene, Nietzsche's
dionysian and apolline, Jung's introvert and extrovert—but
before them all, Schiller's grace and dignity, form impulse and
material impulse, naïve and reflective poetry, realist and idealist.
Those who came after him and tried to add something new to his
analysis sometimes gave up in a mixture of frustration and
admiration—what more was there to say? For Thomas Mann,
who wrestled with antitheses all his life and once vainly tried to
link his entire collection in a single embracing treatise, Schiller's
Naïve and Reflective Poetry came to seem 'the classic German
essay, which really makes all others superfluous since it
contains them in itself'.

It is not of course a matter merely of virtuoso style and of moving conceptual counters about. No one was more convinced than Schiller that in the midst of rhetoric we are in life. To reach worthwhile resolutions means formulating and working through real conflicts. That is the root and value of the dramatic imagination, whether it is creating for the stage or for the forum of thought. When the writer packs contrary energies into the antithetical terms of an argument as when he shapes antagonistic characters within an action, it is not a mere verbal trick. It recognizes—'idealist' though he may be—the structure and texture of the real.

Further reading

1. Translations

PLAYS Schiller's dramas have been translated many times. The only one that seems not to be available in a modern English edition is *The Conspiracy of Fiesco*. Recent translations of the others are: *The Robbers & Wallenstein*, by F.J. Lamport, Penguin Classics, 1979; *Love and Intrigue*, by Frederick Rolf, New York, 1962, *Don Carlos, Wallenstein, The Bride of Messina/ Wilhelm Tell/Demetrius*, and *Mary Stuart/The Maid of Orleans*, all by Charles E. Passage, published by Ungar, New York, in the late 1950s; *William Tell*, translated by John Prudhoe, Manchester, 1970 and by W. E. Mainland, Chicago, 1972; *Mary Stuart* in a free adaptation by Stephen Spender, London, 1959, and in the translation by Schiller's contemporary, Joseph Mellish, revised by Eric Bentley, New York, 1959. A more celebrated contemporary translation is that by Coleridge of *Wallenstein*, edited by Joyce Crick in a forthcoming volume of the Bollingen *Collected Works of Samuel Taylor Coleridge*, general editor Kathleen Coburn, Princeton.

PHILOSOPHICAL AND CRITICAL There are modern translations of *On Naïve and Sentimental Poetry* by Helen Watanabe, Carcanet Press, 1981, and (together with *On the Sublime*) by Julius A. Elias, Ungar, New York, 1966. The Elias version, with some modifications, is reprinted in *German Aesthetic and Literary Criticism*, edited by H. B. Nisbet, Cambridge, 1985, where it is usefully set in context among other key texts of the period by Winckelmann, Lessing, Hamann, Herder, and Goethe. The edition of the *Aesthetic Letters* by Elizabeth M. Wilkinson and L. A. Willoughby, Oxford, 1967, paperback reprint 1982, is an authoritative labour of love, which gives German and English facing texts, an extensive scholarly introduction, a detailed commentary keyed to the English text, a glossary of Schiller's German concepts and, among other appendices, an especially useful one with 'visual aids' to the understanding of Schiller's rhetorical structures. Another scholarly *tour de force*, the product of collaboration between a medical historian and a Germanist, is Kenneth Dewhurst and Nigel Reeves, *Friedrich Schiller: Medicine, Psychology and Literature*, Oxford, 1978. This contains the first complete translation of Schiller's Karlsschule medical writings (including his sole surviving prescription) accompanied by substantial essays on the medico-philosophical background.

HISTORY Translations of Schiller's historical works are not in print. There are versions of *The Revolt of the Netherlands*, by A. J. W. Morrison and L. Dora Schmitz, London, 1897, and of *The History of the Thirty Years War* by Morrison, London, 1899. For an English version of Schiller's Inaugural Lecture on Universal History, see the journal *History and Theory*, 11/3, 1972, pp. 321–34.

POETRY This was much translated in the nineteenth century. Sir Edward Bulwer Lytton, *The Poems and Ballads of Schiller*, London, 1887, was able to capture a good deal of Schiller's tone, which has much in common with Victorian high seriousness.

LETTERS *The Correspondence of Schiller with Körner*, translated by L. Simpson, 3 vols., London, 1849; *The Correspondence between Schiller and Goethe*, translated by L. D. Schmitz, 2 vols., London, 1877.

SELECTION *Friedrich Schiller. An Anthology for our Times*, translated by Jane Bannard Greene and others, Ungar, New York, 1959, repr. 1976.

OPERA As translations in a slightly different sense, the adaptations of Schiller's plays for the operatic stage offer an intriguing angle on his work and a record of his nineteenth-century standing and reception. From *The Robbers* Verdi made *I Masnadieri*, from *Love and Intrigue* his *Luisa Miller* (a return to Schiller's original title), from *The Maid of Orleans* his *Giovanna d'Arco*. The finest of the set is *Don Carlos*, which goes even further than Schiller in interpreting Philip II as a tragic figure (esp. the King's great aria 'Ella giammai m'amò'). Besides Verdi's four operas, there are Donizetti's *Maria Stuarda*, Tchaikovsky's *Orleanskaya Deva* (*Maid of Orleans*), and Rossini's *Guillaume Tell*.

SONG Not many of Schiller's poems found their way into German song, since few of them are in the lyrical mode that invites setting. One or two were set by Liszt and Schumann, and some

114

dozen by Schubert, most of them declamatory rather than melodic. But his setting of 'The Gods of Greece' is ample compensation.

2. *Works on Schiller*

BIOGRAPHICAL The early *Life of Schiller* by Carlyle (1825 and later expanded editions) can still be relished as the response of one master of the grand style to another. A readable modern biography is that of H. B. Garland, London, 1950. In a class of its own for empathetic understanding is Thomas Mann's short story *A Weary Hour (Schwere Stunde)* of 1905, which evokes Schiller's love-envy of Goethe and his victory over despair as he struggles with the composition of *Wallenstein*. Mann's essay *Goethe and Tolstoy* of 1932 (in *Three Essays*, New York, 1932) considers these two authors and their typological opposites Schiller and Dostoevsky in the light of Schiller's own theory of 'naïve' and 'reflective' writers.

HISTORICAL BACKGROUND The early chapters of James Sheehan, *German History 1770–1866*, Oxford, 1989, give a full picture of culture, society, and politics, and of the relations between them. Over half of Adrien Fauchier-Magnan's popular account of *The Small German Courts in the Eighteenth Century*, London, 1958, is devoted to the Duchy of Württemberg, and most of that to the reign of Karl Eugen. The authoritative work on German rulers and their local politics is F. L. Carsten, *Princes and Parliaments in Germany from the Fifteenth to the Eighteenth Century*, Oxford, 1959. For the broader context of eighteenth-century German culture, see W. H. Bruford, *Germany in the Eighteenth Century. The Social Background of the Literary Revival*, Cambridge, 1935.

THEORETICAL AND LITERARY Schiller's aesthetic theories are alive and well in contemporary discussion. They are given a sympathetic reading in Michael Podro, *The Manifold in Perception. Theories of Art from Kant to Hildebrand*, Oxford, 1972, in Anthony Savile, *Aesthetic reconstructions: the Seminal Writings of Lessing, Kant and Schiller*, Oxford, 1987, and more tangentially in the latter author's *The Test of Time. An Essay in Philosophical Aesthetics*, Oxford, 1982. They are drawn, again positively, into a discussion of Marxist thinkers (Ernst Bloch,

Herbert Marcuse, Sartre, and others) in Fredric Jameson, *Marxism and Form*, Princeton, 1971. Their relevance specifically to Marx is studied by Philip J. Kain, *Schiller, Hegel and Marx. State, Society and the Aesthetic Ideal of Ancient Greece*, Kingston & Montreal, 1982. David Meakin's *Man and Work*, London, 1976, contains despite its title a useful survey of later thinkers on 'play' as a key to art and as a social value. J. H. Huizinga in *Homo Ludens. A Study of the Play Element in Culture*, London, 1949, offers a broad historical survey but deliberately avoids issues of psychology and theoretical aesthetics (and from the one reference to the *Aesthetic Letters* seems not to have been aware of the socio-political dimension of Schiller's argument). On the 'perennial' pursuit of the Real in Western literature to which Schiller's *On Naïve and Reflective Poetry* belongs (cf. pp. 77 f.), see Erich Auerbach, *Mimesis. The Representation of Reality in Western Literature*, Princeton, 1953. M. H. Abrams, *Natural Supernaturalism*, London, 1971, traces in masterly fashion the patterns of religious and secular thought which link Schiller and his contemporaries with the English Romantics. The aesthetics of Sublimity in English literature are studied by S. H. Monk, *The Sublime. Critical Theories in Eighteenth-century England*, New York, 1935 and by Marjorie Hope Nicolson, *Mountain Gloom and Mountain Glory: The Development of the Aesthetics of the Infinite*, Ithaca, 1959. On the German literary situation and the influence of Goethe, Schiller, and their associates, see W. H. Bruford, *Culture and Society in Classical Weimar*, Cambridge, 1962. F. J. Lamport, *German Classical Drama: Theatre, humanity and nation 1750-1870*, Cambridge, 1990, devotes several chapters to Schiller's plays, and sets them in their national tradition. On Goethe, see my volume in the present series, Oxford, 1984; and for a fuller picture of Goethe's and Schiller's joint achievement, its origins and significance, T. J. Reed, *The Classical Centre. Goethe and Weimar 1775-1832*, London, 1980, repr. Oxford, 1986.

Index

Index

118

Index